NAHC

Wild Game Cookbook

edited by
Bill Miller, Ron Larsen
Colleen Ferguson

designed by
Dean Peters

typeset by
Amy Sumner

Published by the North American Hunting Club
Minneapolis, MN 55343

We would like to thank the following for their help:

NAHC Members, for sending us more than 200 original wild game recipes for this 1993 NAHC Wild Game Cookbook. These recommended recipes from your fellow NAHC members are the heart of this cookbook.

Wayne and Sherry Fears, for pulling together an extensive and tasty collection of traditional Southern recipes and the lore behind them.

All of the authors who wrote up their best campfire hunting tales as chapter introductions for this book.

NAHC Staff Members, for their long hours in seeing that this project came together in the professional manner in which NAHC Members are accustomed: Publisher Mark LaBarbera, Editor Bill Miller, Managing Editor Ron Larsen, Associate Editor Colleen Ferguson, Art Director Dean Peters, Desktop Publishing Specialist Amy Sumner, Senior Editorial Assistant Debra Morem, Vice President of Product Marketing Mike Vail, Marketing Manager Cal Franklin and Marketing Project Coordinator Laura Resnik.

Cover and inside photos by Wayne & Sherry Fears. Illustrations by David Rottinghaus.

Address reprint requests and orders for additional cookbooks to: NAHC Cookbook Editor, P.O. Box 3401, Minneapolis, MN 55343

Library of Congress Catalog Card Number 84-649847

ISBN 0-914697-46-3
Copyright 1992, North American Hunting Club

The North American Hunting Club offers a line of hats for hunters. For information, write: NAHC, P.O. Box 3401, Minneapolis, MN 55343.

Contents

Steven F. Burke

Great Southern Hunting

When push comes to shove, I would have to say my most successful hunts as far as game bagged have taken place in the northern and western parts of the United States and Canada. As I look at the trophies on the walls around my home and the office, I see moose, caribou, mountain goat, elk, black bear, mule deer, white-tailed deer and more. A lot of animals, but all from north of the Mason-Dixon Line.

That's not to say I haven't hunted in the South. I sure have, and I've enjoyed every trip. Turkey have always put the jinx on me, and the rack of a big Southern whitetail does not yet grace my wall, but you'll never catch me saying that my hunts in the southern U.S. weren't fun.

The hunts I've made in Alabama, North Carolina, South

Carolina, Mississippi and Virginia were each a success in that they introduced me to the finest in Southern hospitality. Any time a "Yankee" heads south to a hunting camp he'll notice one thing right off. Southern hunters have a tremendous respect for tradition.

Each camp has its unique way of "testing" the newcomer. Wide-spread traditions like "bloodying" (smearing blood from a youngster's first deer on the successful hunter's face) are quite common. Viewed from the outside, some of these traditions might seem like gruesome rituals, but they are revered rites of passage in many hunting camps. For example, just as European hunters place a leafy twig in the mouth of a fallen stag and observe a moment of silence, "bloodying" is a sign of respect for and oneness with the game.

Other Southern deer camps include "shirttailin'" among their traditions. This quaint rite is bestowed upon any hunter foolish enough to miss a buck in front of a witness or confess a miss back in camp. In either case the offending hunter is taken to the ground and held there by his "friends." The camp's senior hunter steps forward with Bowie knife in hand, and, with a deft stroke of the shining blade, separates the tail from the rest of the shirt. It matters not if the shirt is a tattered, grease-stained work shirt or an $80 out-of-the-package-that-morning, L.L. Bean custom-hunting shirt. You miss, and the tail goes.

But, the greatest and most universal traditions of all Southern hunting camps are the meals. The food at every Southern camp from which I've hunted was wonderful and plentiful.

NAHC Staff Members always count on losing a little weight when hunting in the mountains or on the tundra, but not on a Southern hunt. If general hunting camp tradition is "three squares a day," then Southern tradition is "three cubes a day"—the meals are huge.

Take for example a typical day at Southern Sportsman Lodge near Montgomery, Alabama:

You wake well before daylight to incredible smells coming from the dining room. As you tie your boots, you can hear the clink of dishes and coffee cups. A buffet awaits you which includes eggs, biscuits and red-eye gravy, grits, toast and all the other accoutrements. Coffee is in great supply along with juice and milk. Conversation over the steaming plates of food is one of the adventures the new day holds.

The guides have you in your stand well before daylight. There's coffee in a thermos and lunch in a sack if you want to stay all day. As noon approaches, you know that the successful hunters and some of the unsuccessful ones are gathering on the front porch of the lodge starting to exchange tales of the morning's hunt as they await lunch. They'll share adventures between mouthfuls of fried chicken, mashed potatoes, fresh vegetables and all the fixin's. You may choose to stay in your stand, but the temptation will be great.

Well after dark, the hunters are assembled in the dining room for the "big" meal of the day. This time the entrees include fresh venison liver, tenderloin and chicken-fried steak. Heaping trays of corn bread dripping with butter are carried in one after another. Dessert, if there's room, is sure to be some regional delicacy like bread pudding with Jack Daniels' sauce.

Then it's to bed to hunt—and eat—all over again. In Southern hunting camp there's something to be said for hunting to work up a bigger appetite for the next outstanding meal.

It's with that tradition in mind that the NAHC staff has prepared the 1993 NAHC Wild Game Cookbook. Of course, it includes recipes from across North America from the Club's 420,000 members, but I think you'll especially enjoy the Southern Cooking portion of the book. Longtime NAHC supporters Wayne and Sherry Fears have put together a mouthwatering section of unique Southern cuisine, including complete wild game dinners with all the fixin's. Whether a trophy is bagged or not, good friends, good food and good times are really what hunting's all about. Enjoy, y'all!

Steve Burke
President

COOKBOOK ABBREVIATIONS

tsp.	=	teaspoon
T.	=	tablespoon
pt.	=	pint
oz.	=	ounce
lb.	=	pound
pkg.	=	package
qt.	=	quart

MEASUREMENT CONVERSIONS

1 pinch	=	less than ⅛ tsp.
1 T.	=	3 tsp.
2 T.	=	1 oz.
4 T.	=	¼ cup
5 T. + 1 tsp.	=	⅓ cup
8 T.	=	½ cup
10 T. + 2 tsp.	=	⅔ cup
12 T.	=	¾ cup
16 T.	=	1 cup

1 cup	=	8 oz.
1 pint	=	16 oz.
1 quart	=	32 oz.
1 gallon	=	128 oz.

1 cup	=	½ pint
2 cups	=	1 pint
4 cups	=	1 quart
2 pints	=	1 quart
4 pints	=	½ gallon
8 pints	=	1 gallon
4 quarts	=	1 gallon
8 gallons	=	1 bushel

Venison

The Traditions Live

by Ronnie (Cuz) Strickland

The night before my first bona fide white-tailed deer hunt was almost as memorable as the hunt. At the tender age of nine, I had already partaken in several species of smaller game such as squirrels, rabbits and doves—standard fare for youngsters in the South. However, deer hunting with my dad was what I was waiting for.

My father was the long-time sportswriter for the local newspaper. His personal tastes leaned more toward the fishing side of things than toward white-tailed bucks, but none the less for my first big-game hunt he had secured a deer hunt on one of the oldest and best deer clubs in Adams County, Mississippi.

I had practiced with my Stevens side-by-side 20 gauge on lots of other game. With money earned and saved from scrounging and selling cola bottles, I purchased buckshot shells for the hunt. All in all, I believed I was ready for the biggest day of my young, hunting-crazed life.

The night before my first deer hunt I must have spent three hours laying out clothes and asking my dad countless questions about deer hunting. On Fridays, I was allowed to stay up late to watch "Shock Theater" which usually consisted of a classic horror tale. I can still remember the movie that night: *The Hounds of the Baskerfields*—a fitting tale for viewing by an impressionable 9-year-old who was about to hunt with hounds in the morning!

I watched the movie until the bitter end. When I was sent to bed, I was still wide awake. I remember tossing and turning for hours and never really falling asleep. All I could think about was bagging my first buck.

When 4:30 a.m. arrived, I was already fully dressed and waiting for my dad. The cold, predawn darkness was even darker because of the thick, threatening clouds that more than hinted of rain. I climbed into our 1961 Dodge pickup (which was missing the passenger-side window) and prepared for the hour-long drive to the Ashland Hunting Club—the place of all my dreams.

Halfway to our destination, a steady sheet of sleet and ice began to fall from the sky. I had to hold my dad's hunting coat over the window to keep the sleet from coming in. By the time we pulled into the camp, my hands were nearly blue.

Once inside the old, stately Southern camphouse, I warmed up next to the huge, open fire. The fireplace mantel was lined with old shirttails that had been removed from hunters' shirts in seasons past. The tradition of cutting off the shirttail of a hunter that misses is still observed in many places in the South.

Breakfast consisted of huge homemade biscuits and tomato gravy with deer sausage and grits. The huntmasters ate at a separate table, and I listened as they discussed the plan for the cold, wet morning hunt.

Venison

"We'll put out down Moss road, and Henry can let the dogs out near Breaux Swamp" was the statement I remember best. I realized that the sleet and ice made no difference to the men at Ashland Hunting Club. This was the big time, and I was right there to enjoy it all.

Dad and I were loaded into "Topless Willy's" Jeep and taken what seemed like 10 miles into the darkness. The huntmaster/ driver knew the roads and woods of this club better than most folks know their own living room.

We finally stopped at what seemed to be just another spot in the endless darkness. The huntmaster told my dad that this spot was one of the best crossings for the morning hunt and that I should have a good opportunity at my first buck. "Keep your eyes open and watch down toward that old live-oak tree," he warned as he pulled off. "Hate to have to add that youngun's shirttail to our wall his first time here!"

Dad, being the true fisherman he was, immediately built a roaring fire to keep warm. I wanted to say that the fire would spook any approaching deer, but I could see that dad was in no mood for my opinion, so I stayed quiet.

For what seemed like hours, we sat by that fire and saw or heard no more than barred owls waking the woods. Then, in the distance arose the faint, but distinct sound of barking dogs. The growing sound came closer and closer. Dad stood up and told me I'd better do the same. In just a few short minutes, the woods went from silence and calmness to total confusion and mayhem. Deer were bounding everywhere.

Dad spotted the buck first. It was in the back of about 15 does, running straight for the big oak tree we were told to watch. "Get your gun up, son, and watch that opening by the tree," he whispered.

I watched the bead on the 20 gauge dive up and down as my heart raced. Then, the buck peeled off and ran even closer to us than the other deer. "Shoot him," dad shouted. And I did, with both barrels of the bobbing 20 gauge.

The 6-pointer ran another 30 yards and fell.

The next few minutes are somewhat cloudy now, but I can remember dad walking to the deer and a big smile coming over his face. "Good shot," were his only words as he looked the buck, then me, up and down. We sat, just being quiet for awhile. I was, I think, in mild shock; stunned by nine years of daydreams and night dreams all coming true in an instant. I think he wanted to just let the seriousness of the moment soak into my young mind.

Shortly the huntmaster pulled up and helped my dad load the buck into the Jeep. At camp, other Jeeps pulled in with several other deer including one wide-racked, heavy-horned, 10-point buck. I will never forget looking at that 10-point buck and thinking I would someday get one that big.

The deer were taken to the cleaning shed where people were already busy dressing the bucks. Dad called me over to where my deer was hanging and put his arm around me. "Son, you did good," was all he said as several other huntmasters took to the task of wiping the blood from the buck on my beaming face.

Now, 30 years later, I still remember the sights, sounds and smells of that first hunt. Many times, I have stood by another fireplace and returned to that morning, realizing how lucky I was to grow up in a house where muddy boots, guns and fishing rods were as common as mom's home cooking.

I now have a family of my own, and my two daughters have had the outdoor experience. Spring turkey and fall whitetails are now a part of their lives. Even if they don't continue their own hunting, they will always understand and accept the need in others to hunt. That tolerance is a tradition that we need a lot more of today.

Venison Chili Con Carne

Serves: 2-4
Prep Time: 1 hour, 15 minutes

1½ **lbs. ground venison**
3 **cups kidney beans,**
   cooked
2 **cups onion, chopped**
1½ **cups tomato soup**

3 **T. chili powder**
3 **T. water**
2 **T. flour**
1 **tsp. salt**

Brown venison in skillet. Add beans, onions and tomato soup and cook for 15 minutes. Add remaining ingredients and cook for 45 minutes or until thick.

Joe Depaolantonio
Colorado Springs, Colorado

Chicago Chili

Serves: 4
Prep Time: 3 hours, 30 minutes

2 **lbs. ground venison**
1 **lb. ground beef**
2 **onions, chopped**
7 **small celery stalks,**
   chopped
2 **green peppers, chopped**
   butter
4 **garlic cloves, pressed**
3 **T. parsley**
3 **T. Worcestershire**
   sauce

3 **T. chili powder**
   garlic salt to taste
   salt and pepper to taste
1½ **cups water**
1 **16-oz. can red kidney**
   beans, drained
1 **16-oz. can pinto beans,**
   drained
1 **15-oz. can tomato**
   puree
2 **T. pepperoni (optional)**

Brown venison and beef in large pot. (Drain if necessary.) In large frying pan, saute vegetables (except beans) in butter until tender. Add all seasonings and water to meat on low heat. Add remaining ingredients and vegetables to pot. Cook on low heat, stirring constantly for approximately 3 hours.

Dave Roman
Chicago, Illinois

Mountain Chili

Serves: 4
Prep Time: 1 hour

2 lbs. venison steak, cubed
1/4 lb. margarine
1/4 lb. vegetable oil
3 tomatoes, chopped
3 green peppers, chopped
1 large onion, chopped
2 dashes Tabasco sauce
2 tsp. chili powder
1 tsp. cumin
3 T. hot pepper relish to taste
1/2 tsp. salt
1/2 tsp. pepper
1 tsp. ground mustard
2 dashes Worcestershire sauce
1 tsp. celery salt
1 12-oz. can tomato soup
1 12-oz. can kidney beans
2 12-oz. cans water

Melt margarine in oil. Saute tomatoes, green peppers and onion until cooked (but crunchy). Then, saute meat until medium. Combine all ingredients. Simmer 30 minutes, stirring constantly.

Roger Plouff
Cape Neddick, Maine

Texas Venison Chili

Serves: 4-6
Prep Time: 40 minutes

2 lbs. ground venison
1 8-oz. can tomato sauce
2 oz. chili pepper
1 oz. oregano
1 oz. paprika
1/2 oz. onion and garlic
1/2 oz. red pepper
1 oz. masa flour

Sear venison in large skillet or saucepan. Add tomato sauce and 2 cans water. Stir in all ingredients (except red pepper and masa flour). Then, add red pepper (half of amount will provide medium-hot chili). Cover skillet and simmer for 30 minutes. Stir. Stir masa flour into 1/4 cup warm water. Add to chili; cook for 15-20 minutes.

Richard Ber
Austin, Texas

Wild Game Chili

Serves: 6
Prep Time: 6-8 hours

1 **lb. ground venison**	2 **T. chili powder**
2 **15-oz. cans kidney**	1 **tsp. salt**
beans	1/2 **tsp. ground cumin**
1 **14¹/₂-oz. can whole**	1/2 **cup picante sauce**
tomatoes, cut up	1 **cup water**
1/2 **cup onion, chopped**	
1/4 **cup green pepper,**	
chopped	
1 **garlic clove, crushed**	

Brown venison in skillet and put in large Crockpot or Dutch oven. Add remaining ingredients and turn on low heat for approximately 6-8 hours.

Kevin Yadon
Belgrade, Montana

Venison Chili

Serves: 6
Prep Time: 3 hours

2 **lbs. ground venison**	1 **28-oz. can tomato**
butter	**sauce**
1 **large onion, minced**	2 **tsp. chili powder**
1 **T. garlic, minced**	**pepper to taste**
1 **large jar picante sauce**	
1 **28-oz. can tomatoes,**	
cubed (use juice, too)	
1 **15-oz. can chili beans**	
1 **can mushroom bits**	
and pieces	

Brown venison in butter. Add onion and garlic and cook for 10 minutes. Add remaining ingredients and simmer for 2-3 hours.

Tim Bacon
Fort Dodge, Iowa

Easy Venison Chili

Serves: 4-6
Prep Time: 40 minutes

1 **lb. ground venison**
1 **pkg. chili seasoning mix**
1/2 **cup water**
1 **16-oz. can kidney beans**

1 **8-oz. can tomato sauce**
6 **Swiss cheese slices**
bacon bits (optional)

Brown ground venison until crumbly. Remove from heat. Add seasoning mix, water, kidney beans and tomato sauce. Mix thoroughly. Bring to a boil while stirring. Reduce heat and simmer for 10-15 minutes (uncovered), stirring occasionally. Ladle chili into microwave bowl. Put slice of Swiss cheese over top and sprinkle with bacon bits. Put in microwave on high for 20 seconds or until cheese melts. (For a spicier taste, add dash of Tabasco sauce.)

Samuel Mears
Onancock, Virginia

Cubed Venison Chili

Serves: 8
Prep Time: 1 hour

2 **lbs. venison, cut into 1/4-inch cubes**
1/3 **cup dried onions**
1/4 **tsp. garlic, minced**
2 **tsp. ground cumin**

2 **T. chili powder**
3 **T. flour**
1 **tsp. salt**
pepper to taste
21/2 **cups tomato juice**

Saute venison with onions and garlic in Dutch oven for about 15 minutes, stirring occasionally. Add cumin, chili powder, flour, salt and pepper; stir. Then, add tomato juice. Cover and cook for another 15 minutes. Uncover and cook for 15 minutes more. Serve hot over preheated chili beans.

Junior Parson
Salem, Oregon

Deer Camp Bean Chili

Serves: 8-10
Prep Time 1 hour, 30 minutes

2 lbs. ground venison
1 cup onion, chopped
1 16-oz. can tomatoes
2 15-oz. cans kidney
beans
1 16-oz. can pork and
beans

salt and pepper to taste
2 tsp. chili powder
2 15-oz. cans tomato
sauce
1 cup beef bouillon (if
needed)

Brown venison with onion and drain grease. Add remaining
ingredients and simmer on low heat for 1 hour. (Water or beef
bouillon can be added if chili is too thick.) Stir occasionally.
Serve with crackers.

Marty Niles
Frederic, Wisconsin

Chili

Serves: 4
Prep Time: 30 minutes

1 pkg. ground venison
(or venison sausage)
3 medium onions,
chopped
1 pkg. hotdogs, sliced
into 1/2-inch pieces
4 T. margarine, butter or
olive oil

3 16-oz. cans brown
baked beans
5 dashes garlic powder
9 dashes red pepper
9 dashes black pepper
1 16-oz. can "sloppy
joe" sauce (optional)

In electric frying pan, thoroughly brown venison, onions and
sliced hotdogs in margarine at 300 degrees. Add beans and
spices. (Add sloppy joe sauce at this time if desired.) Simmer at
200 degrees for a few minutes, or until beans are warm. (This
dish is even better reheated.)

Jim Skalko
Edinboro, Pennsylvania

White River Deer Chops

Serves: 2-4
Prep Time: 15 minutes

4 loin venison chops (½ to ¾ inch thick)
2 tsp. prepared mustard
4 T. bread crumbs
3 T. melted butter
2 tsp. rosemary or Greek spice mixture
4 tsp. Parmesan cheese, grated
3 T. lemon juice

Top each chop with ¼ tsp. mustard. Broil 4-5 minutes. Turn and top each chop with an additional ¼ tsp. mustard. Broil 4-5 minutes. While second side is broiling, combine remaining ingredients. Spread topping on one side of each deer chop and broil and additional 2 minutes.

Dion Luke
Glenwood Springs, Colorado

Barbecued Deer Chops

Serves: 4
Prep Time: 2 hours, 30 minutes

10 venison chops
3 T. butter
1 onion, chopped
1 garlic clove, minced
3 T. vinegar
3 T. lemon juice
3 T. Worcestershire sauce
3 cups catsup
½ cup celery, chopped
1 tsp. salt
½ cup boiling water
½ tsp. dry mustard
½ T. chili powder

Sear chops in skillet and place in roaster. In separate skillet, prepare barbecue sauce: Saute onion and garlic in butter until transparent. Add remaining ingredients. Bring to a boil and simmer for 20 minutes, stirring occasionally. Smother chops with barbecue sauce and bake at 350 degrees for 2 hours. Turn every 20 minutes.

Richard Campbell
Tamaqua, Pennsylvania

Easy Deer Chops

Serves: 4
Prep Time: 2 hours, 15 minutes

6-8 deer chops
½ cup Italian dressing
¼ cup 7-Up soda

Trim chops or steaks. Combine dressing and 7-Up soda for marinade. Place marinade in flat glass baking dish. Turn meat in sauce and put in refrigerator for 1 hour (covered). Turn meat to other side and let sit in refrigerator for another hour. Place chops (undrained) on grill and cook to medium rare.

Robert Karl
Blue Earth, Minnesota

Timbob's Stuffed Venison Chops

Serves: 4
Prep Time: overnight plus 1 hour, 15 minutes

4 butterflied chops or
small steaks
1 pkg. frozen spinach,
chopped
⅓ cup onion, chopped
⅓ cup Parmesan cheese
1 T. garlic powder
½ stick butter, softened
1 egg
⅓ bag bread crumbs

Thaw and drain spinach overnight. Then, combine drained spinach with remaining ingredients (except venison) and mix well. Stuff butterflied or pocket-cut venison. Wrap meat in aluminum foil and cook at 325 degrees for 1 hour, 30 minutes or until done.

Tim Leininger
Idaho Falls, Idaho

Stuffed Venison Butterfly Chops

Serves: 4
Prep Time: 25-30 Minutes

4 butterflied chops   **¹/₂ cup oil**
8 prosciutto ham slices   **¹/₂ cup flour**
4 cheddar cheese slices

Sauce: **1 12-oz can whole peeled**
¹/₄ lb. mushrooms, sliced   **tomatoes**
1 small onion, chopped

Pound butterflied chops. Lay 2 ham slices and 1 cheese slice in each chop. Roll tightly and close with toothpick. Dredge each chop in flour; then, fry quickly in oil. Place meat in oven and bake at 325 degrees for 10 minutes. Remove meat and pour off most of oil into frying pan. Saute mushrooms and onions. Add tomatoes and reduce heat. Season with salt and pepper. Cover chops with sauce.

James Distel
Philadelphia, Pennsylvania

Charbroiled Venison Chops

Serves: varies
Prep Time: 6-8 hours plus 30 minutes

venison chops
¹/₃ cup lemon juice
1 pkg. "Good Seasons"
Italian salad dressing
¹/₃ cup cooking oil

Remove fat from chops. Combine lemon juice, dressing and oil for marinade. (Shake lemon and dressing together well; add oil and shake again.) Marinate chops for 6-8 hours in mixture. Broil on grill for 15-20 minutes or until done.

James King
Royal Oak, Michigan

Jerky

Serves: several
Prep Time: overnight plus 12-24 hours

5 lbs. venison strips
1 bottle soy sauce
1 bottle barbecue sauce
1 box toothpicks

Place meat in pan. Pour bottles of sauces over meat and marinate overnight. Cover bottom of oven with aluminum foil to catch drippings. Stick toothpicks through the ends of meat and hang meat from oven rack. Set oven on lowest setting, and dry meat for 12-24 hours, or until it starts to harden. Do not allow jerky to become brittle.

Jim Skalko
Edinboro, Pennsylvania

Oven-Dried Jerky

Serves: several
Prep Time: 6-8 hours

2 lbs. venison
1/4 cup soy sauce
1 T. Worcestershire sauce
1/2 tsp. pepper
1/4 tsp. garlic powder

1/2 tsp. onion powder
1 tsp. hickory-smoke flavored salt

Trim and discard all fat from meat. Cut meat into 1/4-inch strips and cut across grain. Mix remaining ingredients together. Stir and dissolve as much as possible. Add meat. Mix thoroughly and coat meat well. Let stand 1 hour, stirring occasionally. Cover center of oven racks with aluminum foil. Arrange meat strips on oven racks. Dry at lowest temperature until hard (4-7 hours or overnight, depending on thickness of meat).

J.W. Kauffman Jr.
Susanville, California

Deer Jerky

Serves: varies
Prep Time: 8-12 hours

venison
1 bottle liquid smoke
toothpicks

Cut venison into strips. Soak strips in liquid smoke overnight. Remove meat from liquid smoke and put toothpicks through one end of meat strips. Hang on rack in oven by toothpicks, placing a dripping pan on bottom of oven. Bake at 250 degrees for 4-6 hours. Place in storage container and use as desired.

Roger Young
Camden On Gauley, West Virginia

Hot & Spicy Jerky

Serves: several
Prep Time: 28 hours

3-4 lbs. venison
3/4 cup Worcestershire sauce
1/4 cup soy sauce
1 tsp. garlic salt
1 tsp. onion salt
1 tsp. spicy brown mustard
1/2 tsp. black pepper
1 tsp. chili powder
2 pinches cayenne pepper
1 tsp. Tabasco sauce
1 tsp. ground pickling spice
pinch of allspice, dill seed and ground cloves

Cut venison into 1/4-inch strips. Combine ingredients for marinade. Marinate venison for 24 hours. Place toothpicks through ends of strips. Hang on rack in oven. Place rack at highest setting. Set oven at 150 degrees. Bake for 4-6 hours.

Richard Mirando
Coxsackie, New York

Kevin's Deer Jerky

Serves: several
Prep Time: 2 days

- **3 lbs. venison**
- **1/2 cup soy sauce**
- **1/2 cup Worcestershire sauce**
- **2 tsp. Accent seasoning**
- **2 tsp. salt**
- **2/3 tsp. onion powder**
- **2/3 tsp. pepper**

Cut venison into 3/4-inch strips. Combine remaining ingredients for marinade. Pour marinade over meat and refrigerate (covered) for at least 1 night. Drain and lay strips on cookie sheet. (Place dripping pan on bottom of oven.) Bake at 150 degrees for 6-8 hours, or until meat is dried.

Kevin Yadon
Belgrade, Montana

BBQ Deer Jerky

Serves: several
Prep Time: 24 hours plus 8-10 hours

- **15 lbs. venison steak or stew meat**
- **2 cups barbecue sauce**
- **1 cup water**
- **1/4 cup A-1 steak sauce**
- **1 small onion, minced**

Combine barbecue sauce, water, steak sauce and onion in bowl. Marinate meat in mixture for 24 hours. Place meat on large sheet tray. Bake at 150 degrees for 8-10 hours. Turn meat every 2 hours.

Jerry Brown
Union Lake, Michigan

Danner Deer Jerky

Serves: varies
Prep Time: 24 hours plus 4-6 hours

per lb. of venison used:	¼ **tsp. cayenne pepper**
2 **T. salt**	1 **tsp. garlic powder**
½ **tsp. black pepper**	1 **T. brown sugar**

Place meat strips into glass or plastic container, one layer at a time. Combine remaining ingredients. Sprinkle mixture over meat. Place meat in refrigerator for 24 hours. After 24 hours, dry each piece off with towel. Place in oven at 150 degrees for 4-6 hours, depending on meat thickness.

Lesa Danner
Woodstock, Virginia

Cajun Venison Meatloaf

Serves: 5-8
Prep Time: 2 hours, 15 minutes

2½ **lbs. venison sausage, or ground venison**	1 **tsp. cajun seasoning**
⅓ **lb. crackers, crushed**	1 **tsp. garlic, minced**
2 **large eggs**	1 **tsp. oregano**
1 **small onion, chopped**	1 **tsp. sweet basil**
½ **red pepper, chopped**	1 **tsp. salt**
½ **green pepper, chopped**	
½ **cup hot cajun mustard**	
½ **cup cajun mustard sauce**	
¼ **cup catsup**	
2 **T. soy sauce**	
1½ **tsp. ginger**	

Heat oven to 350 degrees. Mix ingredients together and form into loaf. Bake for 75-90 minutes.

Norman James
Des Moines, Iowa

Anna's Meatloaf Madness

Serves: 4
Prep Time: 1 hour, 30 minutes

- **2 lbs. ground venison**
- **¼ lb. bacon, finely chopped**
- **1 large egg**
- **¼ cup parsley**
- **½ tsp. fresh pepper**
- **1 T. mustard**
- **2 T. ground oatmeal**
- **¼ cup carrots, peeled and ground**
- **2 T. cold water**
- **1 T. Worcestershire sauce**
- **¼ tsp. celery seed**
- **¼ tsp. sage**
- **1 tsp. salt**
- **3 bread slices (white)**
- **¼ cup catsup**

Add bacon to meat. Thoroughly mix all ingredients (except bread and catsup). Add half of catsup. Shape into loaf in bread pan. Spread rest of catsup on top of loaf. Run bread slices under water to dampen and overlap on loaf. Bake at 350 degrees for about 1 hour, 15 minutes. If bread gets too brown, add aluminum foil over top. Remove from oven. Pour off fat (if any). Remove bread, slice meat and serve.

Walter Squier
Portland, Connecticut

Barbecued Venison Meatloaf

Serves: 4-6
Prep Time: 1 hour, 45 minutes

2 lbs. ground venison
1 cup bread crumbs
1 onion, chopped
1 egg, beaten
1½ tsp. salt
¼ tsp. pepper
½ 8-oz. can tomato sauce

Sauce:
½ cup water
3 T. vinegar
3 T. brown sugar
2 T. mustard
2 tsp. brown sugar
2 T. mustard
2 tsp. Worcestershire sauce
1½ 8-oz. cans tomato sauce
1 6-oz. can tomato paste

Combine ingredients (except sauce) and form into loaf. Put in covered pan. Spread ½ can tomato paste over top of meatloaf. Combine ingredients for sauce, including remaining can of tomato paste. Pour sauce over meatloaf. Bake at 350 degrees for 1 hour, 15 minutes. Baste occasionally.

Stanley Lewis
Bealeton, Virginia

Adirondack Meatloaf

Serves: 4-6
Prep Time: 1 hour, 20 minutes

1 lb. ground venison	**bread crumbs**
½ lb. ground beef	**3 T. oil**
½ lb. ground veal	**celery and carrots,**
1 egg	**sliced**
1 tsp. parsley	**1 medium can tomato**
1 tsp. salt	**sauce**
¼ tsp. pepper	

Combine venison, beef, veal, egg, parsley, salt and pepper and mix well. Add bread crumbs until mixture holds loaf form. Heat oil in Dutch oven. Brown meat on all sides. Place celery and carrots around meat. Add tomato sauce. Cover and simmer for approximately 1 hour until vegetables are done. Serve with mashed potatoes.

John Gobiasky
Lake Huntington, New York

Whitetail Meatloaf

Serves: several
Prep Time: 2 hours, 30 minutes

1½ lbs. ground venison	**1 cup water**
2 tsp. salt	**1 cup catsup**
1 tsp. pepper	**½ cup onion, chopped**
1 tsp. celery seed	**½ cup green pepper,**
1½ cups herb seasoned	**chopped**
dressing mix	

Mix all ingredients together thoroughly. Shape into loaf. Bake (uncovered) at 325 degrees for 1 hour. Cover and continue baking another hour. If desired, meatloaf may be topped with extra catsup or canned tomatoes.

Robert Shenk
Columbia, Pennsylvania

Meatloaf

Serves: 6
Prep Time: 1 hour, 40 minutes

3 lbs. ground venison	**2 eggs**
¾ cup Italian bread	**1 tsp. pepper**
crumbs	**1 tsp. garlic salt**
1 cup picante sauce	**bacon strips**
1 cup onion, diced	**catsup**

Combine venison, bread crumbs, picante sauce, onion, eggs, pepper and garlic salt. Form a loaf in baking dish. Cover loaf with bacon strips and catsup. Bake at 350 degrees for approximately 1 hour, 30 minutes.

Tim Bacon
Fort Dodge, Iowa

Italian Venison Meatballs

Serves: 6
Prep Time: 1 hour

2 lbs. ground venison	**1 cup Parmesan cheese,**
1 lb. ground beef	**grated**
3 eggs	**cooking oil**
2 cups flavored Italian	**1 garlic clove, minced**
bread crumbs	**your favorite spaghetti**
1 parsley sprig	**sauce**

In large mixing bowl, combine venison, beef, eggs, bread crumbs, parsley and cheese. Knead until mixed thoroughly. Take meatball mix and roll into size desired. In frying pan, put enough oil to cover bottom of pan. Add garlic clove. Fry meatballs until well cooked on all sides. Add pan drippings into your favorite spaghetti sauce and let meatballs simmer in sauce until ready to serve with pasta.

Paul Blanda
Charlestown, Rhode Island

Meatballs

Serves: 4-6
Prep Time: 1 hour, 30 minutes

1 lb. ground venison	salt and pepper to taste
½ cup onion, chopped	½ tsp. celery seed
2 eggs	(optional)
1 cup stuffing (dry)	1 can cream of
½ pkg. stuffing	mushroom soup
seasoning	1 cup milk
½ cup milk	

Mix together meat, onion, eggs, stuffing, seasoning, milk, salt and pepper and celery seed. Form mixture into balls. Put balls on cookie sheet and refrigerate for 10 minutes. Brown balls in frying pan, then place in casserole dish. Mix mushroom soup and cup of milk together. Pour over browned meatballs. Bake at 350 degrees for 1 hour. Serve with mashed potatoes. Use sauce for gravy.

Irvin Boomgaarden
Trent, South Dakota

4th Of July Special Ribs

Serves: 6-8
Prep Time: 15 hours

2 lbs. venison ribs	1 cup brown sugar
36 oz. barbecue sauce	1 cup hot/spicy mustard
3 cups water	2 T. horseradish

In large, "slow cooker," place barbecue sauce and water. Add brown sugar, mustard and horseradish, mixing until sugar is dissolved. Add ribs from freezer. Set slow cooker on medium heat. Cover and let cook for 12-15 hours. Stir occasionally. Serve hot.

John Vanetta
Hagerstown, Maryland

BBQ Venison Ribs

Serves: 4-6
Prep Time: 2 hours

ribs from 2 deer
1 qt. barbecue sauce
1 cup water
¼ lb. brown sugar

1 cup molasses
bottled hot sauce to taste

Cut ribs into 1-2-inch pieces. Remove large pieces of fat. Cook ribs in covered pan at 350 degrees until you can pull bone from meat. Throw away all fat and juices. Mix your favorite barbecue sauce in water, adding brown sugar, molasses and hot sauce. Pour this mixture over ribs, stirring to get sauce on all ribs. Cover pan and cook for 1 hour, mixing sauce and ribs occasionally. If you want ribs darker, cook with cover off.

George York
Woodbury, Connecticut

Tangy BBQ Deer Ribs—Colorado Style

Serves: 4
Prep Time: 2 hours

5 lbs. venison ribs
1 cup barbecue sauce
¼ cup orange juice

1½ tsp. red pepper
1 12-oz. can beer
water

Mix barbecue sauce, juice and red pepper in Dutch oven. Combine ribs, beer and enough water to cover ribs; bring to a boil and simmer for 45 minutes. Place ribs on greased grill (with or without aluminum foil) on grate. Cook at 375 degrees uncovered (low coals) for 45 minutes or until done, turning ribs and brushing with barbecue sauce mixture. Serve with baked potatoes and corn on the cob.

Dion Luke
Glenwood Springs, Colorado

Boneless Venison Roast

Serves 8-10 (top round) 4-6 (sirloin tip)
Prep Time: 3-4 hours

5 lbs. top round roast or	**Gravy:**
4 lbs. sirloin tip roast,	**remaining pan juices**
boned	**1/3 cup flour**
garlic cloves	**1/3 stick butter or**
salt and pepper to taste	**1/2 cup milk**

Moisten outside of roast. Place roast in shallow roasting pan; fat-side up. Rub outside of meat with garlic cloves. Completely cover roast with salt and pepper (top, bottom and all sides). Roast at 500 degrees for 15 minutes, then reduce heat to 300 degrees and continue roasting for 3-4 hours, or until internal temperature reaches 145 degrees. (Do not cover roast with aluminum foil. Do not add liquid until roast is completely done.) To make gravy, scrape juices from pan, adding liquid until broth is attained. Mix a roux (flour and butter or milk) and thicken broth while slowly heating. Serve with steamed buttered fresh vegetables and red wine.

R.W. Evans
Wheaton, Illinois

Venison Roast With Mushroom Sauce

Serves: 8
Prep Time: 2 hours, 15 minutes

4 lbs. venison roast	**1 onion, sliced**
1 cooking bag	**1/2 can water**
1 10 3/4-oz. can golden	
mushroom soup	

Place roast in cooking bag with all ingredients. Close roasting bag according to instructions and put in shallow roasting pan. Place roast in preheated oven at 350 degrees for about 2 hours. Serve meat sliced with sauce over it.

Dave Roman
Chicago, Illinois

Crockpot Venison Roast

Serves: 6
Prep Time: 10 hours

2 lbs. venison roast	**¼ cup water**
4 potatoes, cubed	**1 T. Worcestershire**
2 carrots, sliced	**sauce**
1 onion, sliced	
salt and pepper to taste	
1 celery stalk, sliced	
1 pkg. brown gravy mix	

Place potatoes, carrots, onion and celery in Crockpot. Season meat with salt and pepper. Place meat in Crockpot. Combine gravy, water and Worcestershire sauce. Pour mixture over meat and potatoes. Cook on low for 10 hours.

Larry Kroeger
Cincinnati, Ohio

Deer Hunter's Roast

Serves: 4-6
Prep Time: 2-3 hours

2-3 lbs. deer roast
1 can cream of celery
  soup
1 can cream of
  mushroom soup
1 large onion, diced
1½ cups water
  salt and pepper to taste

Combine ingredients and pour over roast in roasting pan. Cook at 350 degrees for 2-3 hours or until meat can be separated easily with fork. Season with salt and pepper.

Rick Cooper
Vienna, Ohio

Venison Chuck Roast

Serves: 4-6
Prep Time: 1 hour, 15 minutes

3-4 lbs. roast	**1 can cream of**
garlic salt	**mushroom soup**
1 cooking bag	**several small onions**
1 can cream of onion	**several small carrots**
soup	**several small potatoes**

Season roast with salt, pepper and garlic salt. Place roast in cooking bag in shallow baking pan. Pour in soups, adding 1 can water per can. Add onions, carrots and potatoes. Seal bag and place in preheated oven at 350 degrees for about 1 hour.

Robert Brienza
Scotia, New York

Venison Roast

Serves: 2-4
Prep Time: 8 hours, 30 minutes

1 4-lb. venison roast	**1 tsp. salt**
1 T. soy sauce	**1 tsp. black pepper**
1 T. Worcestershire	**1/2 cup cooking oil**
sauce	**2 cups water**
1/2 tsp. garlic powder	**2 T. flour**
1/2 tsp. onion powder	**1 cup milk**

Combine soy sauce and Worcestershire sauce and rub roast evenly with mixture on all sides. Mix garlic and onion powder, salt and black pepper, and sprinkle evenly on all sides. Heat oil in skillet. Place roast in skillet. Brown on all sides. Remove roast from skillet and place in Crockpot or slow cooker with water. Cover and set heat on high. Cook for 6-8 hours. Remove roast gently and pour broth into small stewer; bring to a boil. Mix flour with milk. Pour mixture slowly into broth using whisk. Stir constantly until consistency is smooth. Serve roast with sauce.

John Salisbury
Green River, Wyoming

Bagged Venison

Serves: 4-6
Prep Time: 3 hours

1 front shoulder	1 can mushroom soup
1 large cooking bag	1 pkg. onion soup mix
1 large onion, chopped	$1/2$ cup water
4 carrots, sliced	$1/2$ cup wine (red or white)
3 celery stalks, sliced	1 bay leaf
3-4 potatoes, cut up	

Season meat with salt and pepper. Place shoulder in cooking bag. Encircle with vegetables. Spread golden mushroom soup over meat. Sprinkle dry onion soup over entire contents. Add water and wine and bay leaf. Once all ingredients are in bag, roll bag around so everything spreads evenly. Preheat oven to 325 degrees. Cook approximately for 2 hours, 30 minutes.

Pete Cuipenski
New Port Richey, Florida

Colorado Ranch Roast

Serves: 3-4
Prep Time: 24 hours plus 3 hours, 30 minutes

1 3-lb. venison eye roast	salt and pepper to taste
$1/2$ cup red wine	$3/4$ cup wild rice stuffing
2 T. soy sauce	$1/2$ orange, sliced
1 cup orange juice	2 T. butter
$1/4$ cup onion, chopped	3 bacon slices
$1/2$ tsp. garlic salt	

Combine wine, soy sauce, orange juice, onion, garlic salt and salt and pepper for marinade. Marinate roast for 24 hours. Remove. Pat dry. Make split in roast and fill with stuffing; tie. Place roast in greased pan. Garnish with orange slices, butter and bacon slices. Roast at 325 degrees for 20-25 minutes per pound. (Baste after 1 hour with marinade.)

John Gobiasky
Lake Huntington, New York

Northern-Fried Deer Steak (Low Fat)

Serves: 3-4
Prep Time: 1 hour

1 lb. venison steaks
1/3 cup flour
1 tsp. light seasoned salt
1/2 tsp. paprika
1/4 tsp. onion or garlic
powder
1/8 tsp. black pepper

1 T. shortening for
frying
1/2 cup water

Use nonstick pan with tight-fitting lid. Combine flour and spices in plastic bag. Shake steaks in mixture (1 or 2 pieces at a time); set aside on waxed paper. Coat all steaks before heating shortening. Heat shortening, then add steak. Brown over medium heat for 2 minutes per side until golden brown. Add water, cover tightly and cook over heat for 30 minutes. Remove cover, increase heat and cook an additional 1-2 minutes. Serve and enjoy.

Robert Gailey
Nezperce, Idaho

Deer Steaks

Serves: varies
Prep Time: 5 minutes

venison steaks
garlic to taste
pepper to taste
flour
vegetable oil

Tenderize steaks. Season steaks with garlic and pepper. Lightly flour steaks on both sides. Brown meat in vegetable oil on medium-high heat. When steaks are lightly brown, they are done.

James Benson
Haines, Alaska

Swiss-Fried Venison Steak

Serves: 3-4
Prep Time: 1 hour, 30 minutes

1 lb. steak, 1 inch thick	**3 tsp. shortening**
1/4 cup flour	**1 cup water**
1 tsp. salt	**3 T. onion, chopped**
1/4 tsp. pepper	**3 T. catsup**

Pound flour into meat on both sides. Season meat with salt and pepper. Heat shortening in frying pan and brown meat on both sides. Add remaining ingredients. Cover and boil for 3 minutes. Then, bake at 325 degrees for 1 hour, basting often.

Denise Reynoldson
Kimball, Nebraska

Marinated Fried Venison

Serves: varies
Prep Time: 8-12 hours

venison, cut into 1/4-inch thin slices	**3 T. steak sauce**
2 T. liquid hickory smoke (or to taste)	**1 pkg. dry onion soup mix**
2 T. Worcestershire sauce	**2 cups water**
	flour
	seasoned salt to taste

In large bowl, mix together ingredients for marinade: liquid hickory smoke, Worcestershire sauce, steak sauce and onion soup mix. Add water. Stir to mix ingredients. Cut venison into 1/4-inch slices. Add meat to marinade. Refrigerate 8-12 hours. (Marinade must cover venison.) When ready for frying, put flour and seasoned salt into brown paper bag. Remove venison from marinade and drop into bag. Shake until well coated. Fry on medium heat until done.

Wilton Sampey
Morgan City, Louisiana

Taco Deer Steak

Serves: 4
Prep Time: 1 hour, 30 minutes

 1 **lb. venison steak**
1½ **cups red wine vinegar**
 2 **cups flour**
   salt and pepper to taste
 ½ **cup shortening**
 2 **8-oz. pkgs. taco cheese**

In large bowl, place venison steak in red wine vinegar and
marinate for 1 hour. Mix flour and salt and pepper together. Put
shortening in large skillet. Remove meat from marinade and roll
in flour mixture. Place meat in large skillet, browning for
approximately 2-3 minutes on each side over medium heat.
After browning all meat, sprinkle taco cheese on top, cover and
simmer for 10-15 minutes or until tender.

Roger Young
Gauley Mills, West Virginia

Venison Filet Mignon

Serves: varies
Prep Time: 15-20 minutes

**venison loin, cut into
2-inch chunks
cracked black pepper**

**garlic powder
bacon strips, smoke-
cured**

Season meat with pepper and garlic powder. On uncut side of
loin, wrap each meat piece with bacon slice, securing with
toothpicks. Place meat on grill with very hot coals (bacon-side
to the fire). Rotate meat when underside (with bacon) turns a
crispy golden brown. When juices begin to come out of the
sides with no bacon, it should be medium rare.

Daniel Hobbs
Wisconsin Rapids, Wisconsin

Stuffed Venison Steak Rolls

Serves: 2
Prep Time: 1 hour, 20 minutes

> **venison steak, cut into**
> **strips**
> **dill pickle slices**
> **flour**
> **salt and pepper to taste**
> **shortening**
> ½ **cup catsup**
> 1 **tsp. Worcestershire**
> **sauce**
> ½ **cup water**

Place pickle on each venison strip. Roll up strip and fasten with string. Then, roll in flour seasoned with salt and pepper. In heavy skillet, heat shortening. Brown venison in shortening. Add catsup, Worcestershire sauce and water. Cover and simmer for 1 hour.

Jeff Stedner
Derby, Connecticut

Deer Supreme

Serves: 4
Prep Time: 1 hour, 15 minutes

> **venison steak**   1 **cup milk**
> **cooking oil**   1 **can sliced mushrooms**
> 1 **can cream of**
> **mushroom soup**

Brown venison in oil and place in casserole dish. Mix soup with milk and pour over meat. Top with mushrooms. Bake at 350 degrees for 45 minutes.

Joe Heatwole
Harrisonburg, Virginia

Venison Ala Park

Serves: 2
Prep Time: varies

venison tenderloin (enough for 2)	**1 small onion, sliced**
⅓ cup red wine	**10 oz. fresh mushrooms, sliced**
⅓ cup Italian salad dressing	**butter**
	blue cheese

Marinate tenderloin in wine and Italian dressing mixture for at least 2 hours. Remove meat from marinade and rub softened butter over it. Broil meat to desired readiness. While venison is broiling, saute onion and mushrooms in butter. Lightly crumble blue cheese over venison. Cover meat with onion and mushrooms. Place in broiler for 1 additional minute.

Tim Leininger
Idaho Falls, Idaho

Arm's Camp Steaks

Serves: 6
Prep Time: overnight plus 2 hours

6 venison steaks	**4 T. olive oil**
1 bottle Italian dressing	**1 pkg. onion soup mix**
1 cup red wine (your choice)	**2 cans cream of mushroom soup**
½ cup flour	**1 can water**

Marinate venison overnight in Italian dressing and wine. Sprinkle some flour on each steak and pound in. (Do the same on the other side.) Heat olive oil in frying pan. Brown steaks in hot oil on both sides. Reduce heat. Sprinkle onion soup mix over meat. In bowl, combine cream of mushroom soup and water. Pour soup mixture over top of steaks. Cover and simmer (turning occasionally) for 1 hour, 30 minutes. Serve with egg noodles, rice or potatoes.

Armand Patnaude
N. Bennington, Vermont

Brandy Pepper Steak With Radishes

Serves: 6
Prep Time: 45 minutes

1½ **lbs. venison steaks,**	**butter**
boned and trimmed	**French brandy**
crushed black pepper	½ **lb. radishes, sliced**

Season steaks with pepper and pound out with meat hammer. In cast iron skillet, melt ½ stick butter and cook steaks over medium-high heat (a panful at a time). When all steaks are done, flash with approximately ⅛ cup brandy per panful. (Be careful not to overdo brandy or wait very long to light—you could get quite a fire or explosion.) Remove steaks and place on serving dish. Repeat until all steaks are done, adding butter as needed. Cook radishes in same manner as steaks; when radishes are opaque, pour over steaks and serve.

Earl Tyler
W. Cornwall, Connecticut

Bennie Bits

Serves: 4-6
Prep Time: 20 minutes

1-2 **lbs. venison steak**	¾ **tsp. each dried parsley,**
1 **egg**	**marjoram, oregano**
milk	**and basil**
1 **cup pancake mix**	**salt and pepper to taste**
cooking oil	**garlic powder to taste**

Trim meat of all fat and silver skin. Cut meat into ½-inch pieces. Mix egg and milk in small bowl. Put pancake mix in plastic bag. Add some of the herb mixture to bag. Sprinkle salt and pepper and garlic powder over venison pieces. Heat oil in large skillet. While heating, place venison pieces in egg and milk. Remove meat and place in bag with coating mix. Shake to thoroughly cover venison. Brown venison on all sides until done.

Dave Roman
Chicago, Illinois

Smothered Venison Stew

Serves: 4
Prep Time: 2-3 hours

1-2 lbs. venison steak, cubed
Adolph's Tenderizer
2 cups flour
salt and pepper to taste
2 T. Mrs. Dash lemon and herb seasoning
1 cup milk
2 T. shortening
1 cup water

Sprinkle meat with tenderizer. Mix flour, salt, pepper and Mrs. Dash seasoning together in pan or bowl. Dip meat in milk, then dredge in flour mixture. In large frying pan, brown meat on both sides in shortening. Add water, cover and bring to a boil. Reduce heat, cover and simmer for 1-3 hours. Make gravy out of left-over flour mix and serve with rice.

Emmett Solomon
Eutaw, Alabama

Joe And Joshua's Venison Delight

Serves: 4
Prep Time: 20-30 minutes

2 lbs. venison steak, cut into 2-inch strips
paprika
1½ tsp. garlic salt
2 beef bouillon cubes
1 cup hot water
2 T. cornstarch
2 large green peppers, sliced
1 large onion, sliced
salt and pepper to taste

Place venison strips in large bowl and cover meat thoroughly with paprika and garlic salt. Brown in large skillet. While browning, place bouillon cubes in hot water to dissolve. Then, add cornstarch. Stir mixture and pour into browned meat. Stir again. Place green peppers and onions over meat. Season with salt and pepper. Cover and simmer for 20-30 minutes. Serve over rice.

Denise Joyce
Steger, Illinois

Texas Stew

Serves: several
Prep Time: 4 hours

- **2 lbs. venison stew meat, cut into cubes**
- **salt and pepper to taste**
- **2 tsp. garlic powder**
- **1 tsp. Tabasco sauce**
- **7 T. Worcestershire sauce**
- **1 16-oz. can peeled tomatoes**
- **1 14-oz. can cajun-style stewed tomatoes**
- **5-6 potatoes, cubed**
- **6-7 carrots, sliced**
- **1 medium onion, chopped**
- **1 tsp. oregano**
- **2 tsp. sugar**

Place meat in large stew pot with enough water to cover. Add salt and pepper, 1 tsp. garlic powder, Tabasco sauce and 5 T. Worcestershire sauce. Bring to a boil. Reduce heat and simmer for 2 hours, adding small amounts of water as needed. After 2 hours, let water boil down to almost no liquid. Add remaining Worcestershire sauce, tomatoes, and 6 cups of water. Bring to a boil. Add potatoes, carrots and onion and reduce heat. Then, add remaining garlic powder, oregano, sugar and salt and pepper to taste. Simmer until vegetables are done, about 1 hour, 30 minutes. Serve with corn bread and Tabasco sauce on the side.

John Lopez
Galveston, Texas

Western Stew

Serves: 4
Prep Time: 6-7 hours

1½ **lbs. venison roast,
    cubed**
 2 **T. oil**
 2 **cups carrots, cubed**
 1 **cup yellow onion,
    chopped**
 1 **cup water**
 2 **cups new potatoes**
 1 **can Mexican stewed
    tomatoes**

 1 **small pkg. frozen corn**
 2 **bouillon cubes**
 2 **T. Worcestershire
    sauce**
   **Mrs. Dash seasoning
    to taste**
   salt and pepper to taste
   garlic powder to taste

Brown meat in oil. Put meat in slow cooker. Add remaining ingredients and stir. Cook on low setting for 6-7 hours.

Earl Leonhardt
West Jordan, Utah

Dilly Venison Stew

Serves: 6
Prep Time: 2 hours

1½ **lbs. venison, cut into
    1-inch cubes**
 ¼ **cup flour**
2½ **tsp. salt**
 1 **tsp. pepper**
 2 **T. shortening**

1¾ **cups water**
 ½ **cup onion, chopped**
 1 **bay leaf**
 ¾ **tsp. dill seed**
 ½ **cup sour cream**

Roll venison in flour mixed with salt and pepper. Brown meat in hot shortening. Add water, onion, bay leaf and dill seed. Cover and cook slowly at low temperature for 1 hour, 30 minutes or until tender. Stir in sour cream and cook only until hot. (Do not boil.) Serve over cooked rice, noodles or mashed potatoes.

Frank Cover
Dunstable, Massachusetts

Brown Venison Stew

Serves: 4-6
Prep Time: overnight plus 2-3 hours

1 lb. venison stew meat	**3 potatoes, diced**
vinegar	**2 onions, diced**
water	**3 carrots, diced**
flour	**1 cup mushrooms**
salt and pepper to taste	**1 small can tomato sauce**
cooking oil	**1 cup raw snap beans**

Soak venison in vinegar and water overnight; then, rinse and dry with clean cloth. Season flour with salt and pepper. Roll meat in seasoned flour. Brown meat in oil, adding water as needed. Cover and simmer until almost tender (about 2-3 hours). Add vegetables and continue to simmer (covered) until vegetables are done. Stir occasionally.

Lewis Gregorich
Bessemer, Pennsylvania

Venison Steak Stew

Serves: 4
Prep Time: 2 hours

2 lbs. deer steak or	**6 potatoes, cut into**
chops	**1-inch cubes**
flour	**3 celery stalks, cut into**
salt and pepper	**1-inch lengths**
shortening	**4 carrots, cut into 1-inch**
McCormicks stew	**pieces**
seasoning mix	**3 small onions,**
3½ cups water	**quartered**

Cut meat into bite-sized pieces. Roll meat in mixture of flour and salt and pepper. Brown meat in shortening. Add seasoning mix and water. Cover and simmer for 45 minutes. Add vegetables and simmer another 30 minutes.

Rick Cooper
Vienna, Ohio

Bailey Venison Stroganoff

Serves: 4-6
Prep Time: 1 hour, 15 minutes

2 lbs. venison cubes
1/4 cup flour
cooking oil
1 cup water
1 cup onions, chopped
2 garlic cloves, minced
1 can mushrooms
2 cans tomato soup

1 T. Worcestershire
sauce
salt and pepper to taste
2 cups sour cream

Shake cubes in plastic bag with flour. Brown in oil. Drain oil from meat. Add water and remaining ingredients (except sour cream). Simmer for approximately 45 minutes. Add sour cream and simmer 15-20 minutes more. Serve over cooked noodles.

Mr. and Mrs. B. R. Bailey
Elizabethtown, Pennsylvania

Venison Stroganoff

Serves 3-4
Prep Time: 30 minutes

1 1/2 lbs. ground venison
3 medium onions,
chopped
cooking oil
2 T. flour
1 can water
1/4 tsp. Worcestershire
sauce

1 can cream of
mushroom soup
1/2 pt. sour cream

Brown meat and onion in oil. Add flour, water and Worcestershire sauce to soup. Blend with meat mixture. Simmer for 15 minutes. Add sour cream. Bring to a boil and serve over cooked rice or noodles.

Charles Gay
Pierson, Florida

Tommy's Barbecued Deer Burgers

Serves: 6-8
Prep Time: 30 minutes

2½ **lbs. ground venison**	4 **T. green onions, finely**
1 **lb. ground beef**	**chopped**
1 **cup soft bread crumbs**	1 **T. salt**
⅔ **cup water chestnuts,**	⅛ **tsp. pepper**
finely chopped	

In large mixing bowl, combine deer and beef with bread crumbs, water chestnuts, green onions, salt and pepper. Shape mixture into 8-10 patties. Combine barbecue sauce, brown sugar, teriyaki sauce and lemon juice. Stir to mix thoroughly and set aside. Place patties 4-5 inches from medium coals. Grill 6 minutes on each side. Baste patties with sauce and grill an additional 3-4 minutes on each side. Serve burgers on Kaiser rolls with any remaining sauce. Burgers can also be broiled.

Tommy Majors
Smithville, Tennessee

Mexican Venison Burgers

Serves: 2-4
Prep Time: 30 minutes

½ **lb. ground venison**	½ **cup water**
cooking oil	1¼ **tsp. salt**
⅓ **cup green peppers,**	**pepper to taste**
chopped	1-2 **tsp. chili powder**
½ **cup onion, chopped**	1 **small can pork and**
1 **6-oz. can tomato paste**	**beans**

In skillet, break venison into small pieces with fork and saute in oil with green peppers and onions until brown. Stir tomato paste into water and add to meat. Add salt, pepper and chili powder. Then, add pork and beans. Stir well and heat until piping hot. Serve over buttered toast with fresh salad or fruit.

Junior Parson
Salem, Oregon

Outdoors Venison Burgers

Serves: 4-6
Prep Time: 1 hour

1½ lbs. ground venison
1½ tsp. salt
⅛ tsp. pepper
 aluminum foil
6 hamburger buns

Combine venison, salt and pepper in bowl, blending well. Shape meat into 12 thin patties. Place a piece of aluminum foil between 2 patties and seal tightly. Place foil on rack 6 inches above hot coals. Grill on both sides until done as desired. Place buns, cut-side down, on rack to toast during last few minutes of grilling. Top with favorite condiments.

James Bradybaugh
Ontario, New York

Mincemeat

Serves: 3 9-inch pies or 5 pts. if canned
Prep Time: 30 minutes or 2 hours, 15 minutes

8 cups ground deer neck
 meat
6 cups apples, peeled
 and chopped
2 cups light brown sugar
1 cup vinegar
2 cups raisins
3 tsp. cinnamon
1 tsp. ground cloves
¾ tsp. allspice

Cook meat until tender. Add apples. Add remaining ingredients. Gradually bring to a boil. (Boil 5 minutes for pies; simmer 2 hours if canning.)

Donald McIntyre
Pleasantville, Pennslyvania

Mouth-Watering Burgers

Serves: 2
Prep Time: 20-30 minutes

2 venison patties	**5 dashes of red pepper**
2 T. olive oil, margarine or butter	**5 dashes of black pepper**
soy sauce	**2 cheese slices**
5 dashes of onion powder	**2 tomato slices**
3 dashes of garlic powder	**4 rye bread slices**
	barbecue sauce

Fry venison in olive oil on one side until deep brown. Turn and do the same to other side. Top with soy sauce and spices and simmer for 1-2 minutes. Serve with cheese and tomato slice on rye bread. Add soy sauce and/or barbecue sauce to taste.

Jim Skalko
Edinboro, Pennsylvania

Venison Bundles

Serves: 2-3
Prep Time: 2 hours, 15 minutes

1 lb. ground venison	**1 cup milk**
⅓ cup milk	**2 T. catsup**
chicken stuffing	**1 T. Worcestershire sauce**
1 can cream soup (any kind)	

Mix venison and ⅓ cup milk together. Shape into flat pancakes. Form stuffing into balls and place in center of venison pancakes. Fold venison around stuffing (so it resembles a softball). Place balls in casserole dish or large pan. Mix soup, milk, catsup and Worcestershire sauce together. Pour this mixture over balls. Bake 2 hours at 350 degrees.

John Keister
Mifflinburg, Pennsylvania

Venison Burger Slop

Serves: 2-3
Prep Time: 40 minutes

1½ **lbs. ground venison**
 2 **cans condensed cream**
   of celery, mushroom
   or onion soup
1½ **cups rice, cooked**

Crumble and saute meat until fully cooked. Pour out juices
and fats. Add your favorite soup. Then, add rice. Mix in pan
and warm.

George York
Woodbury, Connecticut

Blue Cheese Venison Burgers

Serves: 4
Prep Time: 10 minutes

1 **lb. ground venison**	1 **T. Worcestershire**
1 **medium onion,**	**sauce**
chopped	**dash of lemon pepper**
2 **T. butter or margarine**	4 **blue cheese slices**
1 **egg**	**(thin)**
⅓ **cup soft bread crumbs**	4 **hamburger buns**
1 **tsp. garlic salt**	

In large frying pan, saute onion in heated butter until browned;
set aside. Beat egg in medium bowl; mix in crumbs, garlic salt,
Worcestershire sauce and lemon pepper. Combine egg
mixture with venison and onions. Shape into 4 plump round
patties. Cook patties in same pan as onions, browning over
medium heat 4-6 minutes per side turning once. Place blue
cheese strips on each patty after turning to cook second side.
Serve burgers on toasted buns and add your favorite condiments.

Charles Roberts
Mt. Vernon, Washington

Ida's Venison Cacciatore

Serves: 4-6
Prep Time: 45 minutes

2 lbs. venison stew
meat, cubed
fresh black pepper
1-2 T. olive oil
1 cup chianti (red) wine
1 green bell pepper,
sliced

1 medium onion
1-2 garlic cloves, crushed
1 tsp. sweet basil
1 tsp. oregano
1 tsp. rosemary
1 30-oz. can tomato
puree

Season meat with ground pepper. In large Dutch oven or pot, brown venison in olive oil until tender. Add wine and simmer with lid partially open until meat is "dry." Add remaining ingredients. Cover pot and bring to a boil. Then, simmer for 30 minutes with lid partially open.

Paul King
Woodbridge, Virginia

King's Venison Yaki-Tori (hors d'oeuvre)

Serves: 200 hors d'oeuvres
Prep Time: 2-3 days plus 15 minutes

2 lbs. venison strips

Marinade:
¾ cup Saki wine
½ cup soy sauce
1 onion, chopped

2 garlic cloves, chopped
1 tsp. ginger powder
1-2 T. brown sugar

Slice venison into ¼-inch thick strips, approximately 1 inch wide and 2 inches long. Combine marinade ingredients. Marinate strips in covered bowl for 2-3 days in refrigerator. Thread each piece of venison onto 6-inch bamboo skewer. (Skewers are usually sold 100 to a packet). Keep skewers on platter in refrigerator until ready to cook. Grill each skewered strip on small charcoal grill over low heat, turning frequently.

Paul King
Woodbridge, Virginia

Mary's Venison Pizza Topping

Serves: 4
Prep Time: 20 minutes

1 lb. ground venison
1 small onion, chopped
1 garlic clove, minced
1-2 T. olive oil
fresh black pepper

In large skillet, saute onion and garlic in olive oil until tender. Season venison with ground pepper. Add venison to skillet (stirring to break up lumps) and brown. Drain fat from meat. Use topping with your favorite pizza recipe.

Paul King
Woodbridge, Virginia

Venison Hot Dish

Serves: 2-3
Prep Time: 2 hours, 15 minutes

1 lb. ground venison
1 cup celery, diced
1 cup onion, diced
3/4 cup water
3/4 cup catsup
1 tsp. celery seed
2 garlic cloves, minced
1 bunch carrots
1 can kidney beans

Cook meat, celery and onion until meat is separated. Add water, catsup, celery seed and garlic. Simmer for 1-2 hours. Have carrots partly cooked and simmer until they are done. Add beans during last 10 minutes.

Denise Reynoldson
Kimball, Nebraska

Hearty Venison Bake

Serves: 4-6
Prep Time: 45 minutes

- 1 **lb. ground venison**
- 2 **cups mashed potatoes (prepared)**
- 1/3 **cup butter or margarine, melted**
- 1/2 **cup onion, chopped**
- 2 **tsp. Worcestershire sauce**
- 1/2 **tsp. salt**
- 1/8 **tsp. pepper**
- 2 **eggs**
- 1 **cup cottage cheese (small curd)**
- 2 **medium tomatoes, sliced**
- 1 **cup cheddar cheese, shredded**

Heat oven to 350 degrees. In medium mixing bowl, combine potatoes and butter; mix well. Set aside 1/2 cup potato mixture. Spread remaining potato mixture in ungreased 9-inch square baking dish; set aside. In medium skillet, cook meat and onion over medium heat (stirring occasionally) until meat is no longer pink and onion is tender. Drain, if necessary. Stir in Worcestershire sauce, salt and pepper. Spoon onto potato mixture in baking dish. In small mixing bowl, blend eggs and cottage cheese; pour over meat mixture. Top with tomato slices. Sprinkle with cheddar cheese. Spread with remaining potato mixture. Bake (uncovered) until set, about 20 minutes.

Denise Reynoldson
Kimball, Nebraska

Venison Polish Sausage

Serves: several
Prep Time: varies

3 lbs. venison, trimmed and cubed	**5 tsp. salt**
1 lb. beef fat	**2 tsp. pepper**
1 lb. lean pork, cubed	**4 tsp. marjoram**
	3 tsp. garlic powder

Grind meats separately. Knead together and grind again. Sprinkle seasonings on meat, knead it with your hands, then grind a third time. Stuff into casing links or rings. Place formed sausage in rectangular cake pan. Cover sausage with water, and bake at 350 degrees until water has evaporated. Wrap and freeze.

Denise Reynoldson
Kimball, Nebraska

Venison Breakfast Sausage

Serves: several
Prep Time: 30 minutes

1 lb. venison, trimmed
6 oz. lean bacon ends or slab bacon
3/4 tsp. salt
1 tsp. dried sage leaves, crushed
1/2 tsp. ground ginger
1/4 tsp. pepper

Cut meat and bacon into 3/4-inch cubes; place in medium mixing bowl. In small bowl, combine salt, sage, ginger and pepper. Sprinkle seasonings over meat; mix well. Chop or grind meat to desired consistency. Shape meat into thin patties and fry over medium heat until browned, turning once. Sausage can also be frozen uncooked.

Denise Reynoldson
Kimball, Nebraska

Venison Sausage—Italian Style

Serves: 10
Prep Time: overnight plus 15 minutes

5 lbs. venison, fat and gristle removed
1 lb. salt pork
5 T. Morton's sausage and meatloaf seasoning

3 T. fennel seeds (whole)
butter or margarine

Cube venison and salt pork and place evenly on shallow tray. Sprinkle seasonings over meat. Refrigerate (lightly covered with plastic wrap) overnight. Grind meat coarsely and shape into patties. (Patties should be loose, not flattened.) Fry in butter or margarine until done to your liking.

William Heins
Red Bluff, California

Timbob's Venison Sausage

Serves: 9-12
Prep Time: 2 hours, 30 minutes

3 lbs. polish or smoked German venison sausage
1 cup catsup
1/2 cup cider vinegar

1/2 cup sugar
1/2 cup onion, chopped
12 oz. beer
1 T. Worcestershire sauce

Cut raw sausage into bite-sized pieces. Place sausage in Crockpot (or similar sized saucepan). Add remaining ingredients. If using Crockpot, cook on low setting for 2 hours or until done. If cooking on stove, cook on low heat for 45 minutes. (If thicker sauce is desired, leave uncovered during half of cooking time.)

Tim Leininger
Idaho Falls, Idaho

Deer Summer Sausage

Serves: makes 4 sticks
Prep Time: 24 hours plus 6 hours

**1 lb. ground venison
(beef fat added)
1 tsp. Morton's Quick
Cure**

**1 tsp. black pepper
red pepper to taste
garlic powder to taste**

Add Quick Cure and black pepper to meat. Season with red pepper and garlic powder. Mix well. Roll meat into sticks about 1¾ inches long. Wrap in aluminum foil and refrigerate for 24 hours. Bake at 225 degrees for 6 hours. (Add 15 minutes cooking time for each additional 4 sticks.) Let meat cool completely before slicing.

Joe Heatwole
Harrisonburg, Virginia

Opening-Day Hunter's Boiled Smoked Sausage

Serves: 4-6
Prep Time: 12 hours plus 10-15 minutes

**3 lbs. smoked venison
sausage
1 pt. whiskey
2 large onions, sliced
1 potato per person,
chopped into quarters
2 large carrots, chopped
or sliced**

Cut sausage into 4-inch lengths and place in slow cooker or Crockpot. Add remaining ingredients and cover. Let marinate all night. In the morning, turn Crockpot on and simmer for 6-8 hours. Serve on hotdog buns or sliced bread.

Steve Merrell
Pontiac, Michigan

Venison Potato Sausage

Serves: varies
Prep Time: 40-50 minutes

1½ **lbs. venison**	1 **tsp. salt**
1 **lb. pork**	1 **tsp. allspice**
6 **cups potatoes, ground**	1 **tsp. pepper**
1 **onion, ground**	

Mix all ingredients thoroughly. Put mixture into casings and tie off with string. Put in large kettle with enough water to cover. Cook 30-40 minutes, then freeze or refrigerate.

Kevin Slater
Harrison, Nebraska

Venison Fingersteaks

Serves: 4-6
Prep Time: 45 minutes

2-3 lbs. venison, cut into ½-inch cubes
2 **tsp. shortening or oil**
salt and pepper to taste
onion powder to taste
Season All to taste
3-4 **eggs**
1½ **cups flour**

Put venison into frying pan with shortening or oil. Season with salt, pepper, onion powder and Season All. Fry until brown, let cool. Put eggs into bowl and slightly beat. Put flour in another bowl with generous amount of salt, pepper, onion powder and Season All. Stir flour and seasoning together. Combine cooled venison with eggs. Stir and place into flour mixture until covered with flour. Shake off excess flour and put into hot oil or deep-fat frying pan. Fry until brown.

Steve Ryals
Boise, Idaho

Breaded Venison Fingersteaks

Serves: 4-6
Prep Time: 1 hour, 30 minutes

2 lbs. venison	**salt**
1 cup olive oil	**cayenne pepper**
1 cup soy sauce	**garlic powder**
1 qt. peanut oil	**onion powder**
2½ cups flour	

Cut meat into 3-inch strips. (Cut across grain to make more tender.) Soak venison strips in olive oil and soy sauce for about 1 hour. Put peanut oil in deep frying pan. Heat to 350 degrees. Take meat strips out of olive oil and soy sauce. Put into bowl of flour. Add seasonings to taste and mix meat strips in flour. Drop in peanut oil and fry until strips float.

Robert Bisso
Memphis, Tennessee

Vermouth Venison

Serves: 4-6
Prep Time: 1 hour, 15 minutes

2 lbs. venison, cubed	**1½ tsp. sweet basil**
1 cup rice (uncooked)	**1 T. ground ginger**
cooking oil	**1 tsp. garlic, minced**
1¼ cups sweet vermouth	**1 T. black pepper**
2 16-oz. cans Italian	**½ tsp. salt**
stewed tomatoes	**1 sweet pepper, chopped**
1 onion, chopped	

Begin cooking rice. Brown meat in hot oil, then reduce heat to 200 degrees. Add ¾ cup vermouth and juice from stewed tomatoes. Put in onions and add all dry ingredients. Simmer for 10-15 minutes. Add 2 cans stewed tomatoes and red or green pepper. Simmer another 15 minutes. Add remaining vermouth. Add rice to meat (or serve on the side) and cook another 15 minutes.

Norman James
Des Moines, Iowa

Venison Microwave Lasagna

Serves: 4-8
Prep Time: overnight plus 1 hour

1 lb. ground venison	$1/4$ cup Parmesan cheese
1 16-oz. jar spaghetti	1 egg
sauce	1 T. parsley flakes
1 T. dried parsley	1 tsp. basil
1 tsp. dried oregano	8 lasagna noodles
16 oz. cottage cheese	mozzarella cheese

Cook meat 5-6 minutes; drain. Stir in spaghetti sauce, parsley and oregano. Cook 3-4 minutes. Mix cottage cheese, Parmesan cheese, egg, parsley flakes and basil. Spread 1$1/3$ cups sauce in 12x7x2-inch pan. Overlap noodles (4) on sauce. Add mozzarella cheese. Repeat layers. Top with remaining sauce; refrigerate overnight. Cover pan with plastic cling wrap and cook in microwave on high for 10 minutes. Rotate dish and cook on medium for 20-28 minutes. Sprinkle with remaining mozzarella and 3 T. Parmesan cheese. Cover and let stand for 10 minutes.

Kenneth Haydysch
Crystal Lake, Illinois

Quick And Easy Lasagna

Serves: 6
Prep Time: 1 hour

1 lb. ground venison	1 15-oz. jar spaghetti
6 oz. lasagna noodles	sauce
1 onion, chopped	1 cup cottage cheese
cooking oil	(small curd)
$1/4$ tsp. dried oregano	1 pkg. mozzarella cheese

Cook noodles in salted water. Brown meat and onion in oil. Drain. Add oregano and sauce to meat. Simmer for 15 minutes. Layer noodles, cottage cheese, meat sauce and mozzarella cheese in pan. Repeat. Bake at 375 degrees for 30 minutes.

Larry Kroeger
Cincinnati, Ohio

Venison Irish Dublin

Serves: 4-8
Prep Time: 1 hour

1/2 **lb. ground venison**	1 **can cream of**
1/2 **lb. ground beef**	**mushroom soup**
potatoes	1/2 **tsp. thyme**
1 **small onion, chopped**	**cheddar cheese,**
1 **pkg. frozen spinach**	**shredded**
8 **oz. sour cream**	

Cook potatoes, mash, and set aside to cool. Steam onion until done. Add meat and fry until brown; drain. Cook and drain spinach, then add to meat. Add sour cream, soup and seasonings. Heat 10-15 minutes. Line edge of 9x11-inch rectangular pan with mashed potatoes making a wall. Pour mixture into pan. Sprinkle cheese on potato wall. Bake at 350-375 degrees for 10 minutes.

Kenneth Haydysch
Crystal Lake, Illinois

Venison Casserole Supreme

Serves: 6
Prep Time: 1 hour, 30 minutes

2 **cups venison, chopped**	1 **can cream of**
and cooked	**mushroom soup**
1 1/4 **cups spaghetti**	1/2 **cup chicken broth**
1/4 **cup pimiento, diced**	1 3/4 **cups sharp cheddar**
1/4 **cup green pepper**	**cheese, grated**
1/4 **cup onion**	1 **cup sliced mushrooms**

Cook spaghetti and drain. Place meat, pimiento, green pepper and onion in 1 1/2-qt. casserole dish. Pour soup, broth, cheese and spaghetti in casserole. Add salt and pepper to taste. With two forks, toss lightly. Add mushrooms. Sprinkle cheese on top. Cover and bake for 45 minutes until it bubbles.

Richard Ber
Austin, Texas

Meal In One

Serves: 6
Prep Time: 2 hours

1 lb. ground venison	1 small can string beans
1/2 cup onions, chopped	1 small can tomato sauce
1/2 cup bell peppers, chopped	salt and pepper to taste
1 small can mushrooms	1/2 tsp. chili powder
1 small can corn	1 tsp. Worcestershire sauce

Brown ground venison, onions and bell pepper in oil. Add mushrooms. Cook until tender. Drain corn and beans. Add corn, beans and tomato sauce to meat. Mix all ingredients and put in dish. Bake at 375 degrees for 45 minutes.

Emmett Solomon
Eutaw, Alabama

Ground Venison Supreme

Serves 10-12
Prep Time: 1 hour, 30 minutes

2 lbs. ground venison	6 American cheese slices
1 pkg. dry onion soup	2 cans tomato soup
1 10-oz. pkg. frozen peas	1/4 cup water
2 1/2 cups noodles, cooked	1 cup margarine
1 can cream of mushroom soup	3 cups Ritz crackers
1/4 cup milk	1/2 cup cheddar cheese

Brown venison; drain and add onion soup mix. Spread meat mixture in 9x13-inch pan. Sprinkle peas over. Drain noodles and put on top of peas. Mix mushroom soup and milk; pour over noodles. Lay cheese slices over soup. Mix tomato soup and water and pour over cheese slices. Mix melted margarine and Ritz crackers. Sprinkle over tomato mix. Top with cheese. Bake at 300 degrees for 1 hour.

Lynn Horst
Myerstown, Pennsylvania

Mmmpossible Venisonburger Pie

Serves: 6-8
Prep Time: 1 hour

1 **lb. ground venison**	3 **eggs**
1/2 **cup onion, chopped**	2 **tomatoes, sliced**
1/2 **tsp. salt**	1 1/4 **cups cheddar or**
1/4 **tsp. pepper**	**American cheese,**
3/4 **cup Bisquick mix**	**shredded**
1 1/2 **cups milk**	

Heat oven to 400 degrees. Grease 10x1 1/2-inch pie plate. Cook venison and onion in 10-inch skillet until venison is brown; drain. Stir in salt and pepper. Spread meat mixture into pie plate. Beat Bisquick, milk and eggs with wire whisk or hand beater until almost smooth, about 1 minute. Pour over venison in plate. Bake 25 minutes. Remove from oven and top with tomatoes and cheese. Return to oven and bake. When a knife is inserted in the center and comes out clean (about 5-8 minutes), it's done. Garnish with lettuce if desired.

Lynn Horst
Myerstown, Pennsylvania

Stuffed Peppers

Serves: 4
Prep Time: 45 minutes

3/4 **lb. ground venison**	4 **medium green peppers**
1/4 **lb. ground pork sausage**	1 **cup uncooked instant**
1 **16-oz. can stewed**	**rice or 2 cups regular**
tomatoes	**rice, cooked**

Brown venison and pork sausage thoroughly in skillet and drain. Cut peppers in half and clean. Remove meat from skillet and place peppers in skillet with 1/2 cup tomato juice from can. Cover and steam for 10 minutes. Add meat, stewed tomatoes and rice. Season to taste. Fill peppers and steam for 20 more minutes.

Mr. and Mrs. B. R. Bailey
Elizabethtown, Pennsylvania

Smoked Venison

Serves: several
Prep Time: overnight +15 minutes or overnight + 8 hours

1 venison roast, boned
Morton's Tender Quick

Rub roast with Tender Quick. Let stand overnight. For hot main dish, fast smoke meat over hot charcoal. Serve hot off grill. For cold appetizers or sandwiches, cold smoke for about 8 hours.

Dave Crowther
Bluemont, Virginia

Cajun Venison Subs

Serves: 6
Prep Time: 1 hour, 30 minutes

1½ lbs. boneless venison	**cajun spices**
2 8-oz. cans mushrooms	**2 T. cooking oil**
1 cup celery, chopped	**4 beef bouillon cubes**
1 cup green onions,	**6 hoagie buns**
chopped	**12 provolone cheese**
1 T. oil	**slices**

In large skillet, cook sliced mushrooms, celery and onions in oil until almost tender, but not brown. Cut venison into thin slices and pound with grooved side of meat mallet. Sprinkle cajun spices on both sides of meat. Divide vegetables evenly among venison pieces. Spread to within ½ inch of edge. Roll up, starting from one of the short sides, tucking in the sides. Tie with string or fasten with toothpicks. In skillet, brown rolls in hot oil. Drain fat. Add enough water to cover meat. Add bouillon cubes and bring to a boil. Reduce heat, cover and simmer for 1 hour, 30 minutes. Remove string or toothpicks. Thinly slice and serve on buns with juices. Lay 2 provolone cheese slices over meat.

Wayne Strandquist
Clewiston, Florida

Leg Of Venison

Serves: several
Prep Time: 2-3 days plus several hours

5-6 lbs. venison leg
½ cup butter
1 onion, chopped
1 cup red wine
2-3 lumps sugar
½ cup flour
1 cup sour cream
salt and pepper to taste
1 bunch green onions
3 whole cloves

Marinade:
1½ qts. white wine
2 cups vinegar
2 cups olive oil
¼ lb. carrots, sliced
¼ lb. onions, sliced
2 celery stalks, chopped
2 garlic cloves, minced
3 parsley sprigs,
minced
1 bay leaf
peppercorns
3 whole cloves

Soak venison for 2-3 days in marinade. Remove meat and wipe dry with cloth. Melt butter and brown meat evenly on all sides. Fry onion in same butter. Stir in 1 cup of marinade, red wine and sugar. Cover tightly and simmer for several hours until meat is tender. Strain sauce, thicken with flour and add sour cream. Season with salt and pepper. Cut meat in slices and pour sauce over them. Garnish with green onions and cloves, lightly browned in butter. Serve with boiled potatoes.

Ken Powell
Kenosha, Wisconsin

Deer In Tears

Serves: 3-5
Prep Time: 1 hour, 30 minutes

2 lbs. ground venison	**2 tsp. white vinegar**
1/2 lb. pork sausage	**1 T. Worcestershire**
1/4 cup bread crumbs	**sauce**
garlic to taste	**salt and pepper to taste**
1 cup green peppers,	**5 large whole onions**
diced	**butter slabs**

Combine venison, pork sausage, bread crumbs, garlic, green pepper, white vinegar and Worcestershire sauce. Season with salt and pepper. Hollow out onions and stuff with ingredients. Put onions in pan and top with butter slabs. Cover pan and bake at 325 degrees for 40 minutes. For outdoor cooking, wrap stuffed onions in aluminum foil and put under hot coals for about 45 minutes or so. (Check once to test for doneness.)

John Davies
Hanover, Maryland

Venison Tacos

Serves: 4
Prep Time: 30 minutes

1 1/2 lbs. ground venison	**1/4 tsp. onion powder**
2 tsp. ground red pepper	**1/4 tsp. garlic powder**
1 tsp. chili powder	**1/4 tsp. black pepper**
1 tsp. paprika	**1 8-oz. can tomato sauce**
1/2 tsp. thyme	**red hot sauce**
1/2 tsp. cumin	**taco shells**

Mix all dry seasonings together. Brown meat in skillet. Drain off excess oil. Add seasoning mix and tomato sauce. Reduce heat and simmer uncovered for 10 minutes. Add red hot sauce to taste. Put meat mixture on taco shells and add all your favorite toppings.

Ashley Brennan
Garrison, New York

Sauerbraten

Serves: varies
Prep Time: 2 days plus 1-6 hours

> **venison roast**
> **flour**
> **olive oil**
> 1 **small onion, finely**
> **chopped**
> **raisins**
> **sugar to taste**

Marinade:
> 1 **cup cider vinegar**
> 1½ **cups water**
> 1 **medium onion, sliced**
> 2 **bay leaves**
> 6 **cloves**
> 12 **peppercorns**
> 1 **T. paprika**
> 2 **tsp. salt**

Mix all ingredients for marinade. Heat, but do not boil. Put hot marinade and meat in oven roaster bag and refrigerate for at least 2 days. (Make sure entire roast stays in marinade.)

When ready to cook, drain meat and save marinade. Coat meat with flour and brown in olive oil with onion. Put roast and marinade back in roasting bag. Simmer at 250-300 degrees until meat falls apart (about 1 hour per pound).

Remove roast and keep hot. Strain marinade and make gravy. Add raisins and sugar to gravy. Serve with red cabbage and potatoes (or spatzel).

Dave Crowther
Bluemont, Virginia

Australian Rissoles

Serves: varies
Prep Time: 2 hours, 15 minutes

1½ lbs. ground venison
3-4 bread slices
  milk
4-5 bacon slices, minced
  1 large tomato, minced
  1 large onion, minced
  assorted spices and
  herbs of choice
  catsup
  Worcestershire sauce
  flour

Cut crust from bread and break into small pieces, putting them in large bowl. Splash in enough milk to make bread very wet. Add bacon, tomato and onion. Add your favorite herbs and spices, plus a splash of catsup and Worcestershire sauce. Stir into mush. Break meat into small pieces and add to mixture. Mix very thoroughly. (Squish mix through your fingers repeatedly until a uniform mixture results.) Heat pan to 375 degrees. Add a little cooking oil. Roll mixture into about 9 or 10 balls. Roll balls in flour and place in pan (flatten slightly). Cook until dark brown underneath, then turn and reduce heat to 275-300 degrees. Cook until dark brown on that side too, about 30-45 minutes. Drain thoroughly and serve with vegetables.

Graham Wyatt
Mesa, Arizona

Venison Roll-Ups

Serves: 3-4
Prep Time: 1 hour, 30 minutes

3 lbs. venison steak	**salt and pepper to taste**
1 onion, minced	**flour**
bacon, minced	**2 bay leaves**

Cut venison steaks into 3x4-inch pieces (¼ inch thick). Fill steaks with onions and bacon. Then, season with salt and pepper. Roll steaks and secure with toothpicks. Dredge steaks in flour and brown on all sides. Then, add boiling water (to almost cover). Add bay leaves and cook for about 1 hour or until tender. Thicken gravy and serve.

Kevin Slater
Harrison, Nebraska

Venison Enchiladas

Serves: 6-12
Prep Time: 1 hour

1 lb. ground venison	**2 cans enchilada sauce**
½ medium onion, chopped	**12 corn tortillas**
cooking oil	**½ lb. sharp cheddar cheese, grated**
6 black olives, chopped	**4 green onions, chopped**
salt and pepper to taste	

In skillet, saute venison and onion in oil until meat is browned and onion is cooked thoroughly. Stir in olives. Season with salt and pepper. Heat enchilada sauce in large, round pan. Dip each tortilla in hot sauce, removing almost at once. Place tortillas on flat surface. Spoon 1 T. of meat mixture on each tortilla, roll up, and place in greased 9x14-inch baking dish. Make single layer in dish and top with cheese and green onions. Bake for 15-20 minutes at 375 degrees.

Kevin Slater
Harrison, Nebraska

Buck Kabobs

Serves: 8
Prep Time: overnight plus 15 minutes

   3 lbs. venison, cut into 1-inch cubes
   $1/2$ cup oil
   $1/4$ cup vinegar
   $1/4$ cup catsup
   $3/4$ cup yellow onion, chopped
   $3/4$ tsp. salt
   $1/2$ tsp. oregano
   $1/4$ tsp. basil
   $1/4$ tsp. ground pepper
   2-3 garlic cloves, pressed
   2 T. Worcestershire sauce
   green peppers
   tiny onions (or large quartered)
   cherry tomatoes
   mushrooms
   squash slices

In large bowl, combine oil, vinegar, catsup, onion, salt, oregano, basil and ground pepper. Blend in garlic and Worcestershire sauce. Add venison cubes and toss to coat meat. Let soak overnight.

On skewers, alternate venison cubes with vegetables. Broil 5 inches away from heat for 5 minutes per side or until meat is done. On barbecue grill, cook 5 inches above hot coals. Turn often until done.

For Hawaiian style: Add 2 T. pineapple juice to marinade. Use soy instead of Worcestershire and use pineapple chunks on skewers. Serve on rice.

Walter Squier
Portland, Connecticut

Venison Goulash Soup

Serves: 4-6
Prep Time: 30 minutes

4 venison shanks, cut into thirds	**4 T. paprika**
	3 bay leaves
2 qts. tomato juice	**2 garlic cloves, finely chopped**
3 lbs. onions, sliced and sauteed (optional)	**1 T. ground cinnamon**
1/8 cup soy sauce	**1 tsp. nutmeg**
1/8 cup steak sauce	**cayenne pepper to taste**

Place venison and tomato juice in stock pot or large pan. Bring to boil and skim surface. Let cool, allowing fat to come to surface. Add remaining ingredients and simmer until meat falls off bones. Remove bones, bay leaves and cinnamon. Serve over egg noodles, rice, or as soup with heavy bread for sopping.

Dave Crowther
Bluemont, Virginia

Little Meat Sandwiches

Serves: several
Prep Time: 30-35 minutes

1 lb. ground venison	**1 lb. Velveeta cheese**
1 lb. sausage (hot)	**1 tsp. garlic**
1 onion, chopped	**1 tsp. red pepper**
cooking oil	**2 loaves party rye bread**

Brown meat and onions in oil and drain. Add remaining ingredients (except bread). Cook slow until cheese melts. Spread on bread. Freeze on cookie sheet for 5 minutes. Put in bag and freeze. Use as needed. Bake at 350 degrees for 5-6 minutes until cheese melts.

Larry Kroeger
Cincinnati, Ohio

Scott's Sweet And Sour Venison

Serves: 2-3
Prep Time: 1 hour

2 venison steaks
1 tsp. onion, minced
6 T. brown sugar
2 T. yellow mustard
6 T. Worcestershire
sauce
salt and pepper to taste

1/2 cup corn syrup
5 carrots, sliced and
cooked

Cook venison steaks with onion until almost done. Mix remaining ingredients (except carrots) and pour over steaks. Add carrots and simmer (covered) for approximately 20 minutes. Serve with mashed potatoes.

Scott Mould
Cohoes, New York

Klinck's Venison Pancakes

Serves: 4-5
Prep Time: 30 minutes

1/2 lb. ground venison
1 medium onion, diced
1/2 chili pepper, finely
chopped
2 cups mashed potatoes
8 oz. creamed corn
cornmeal

Combine all ingredients (except cornmeal) and form into patties. Sprinkle cornmeal on both sides of patties. Fry patties in greased skillet on medium heat. Flip several times and cook until done. Serve hot with homemade chutney.

Chip Klinck
Hillsboro, New Hampshire

Deer On A Spear

Serves: 4
Prep Time: overnight plus 1 hour

3 lbs. venison	**8 oz. sherry wine**
2 cups green onion, chopped	**1 large onion, cubed**
	cherry tomatoes
2 T. garlic powder	**Italian squash, cubed**
½ cup parsley	**bamboo skewers**

Cut venison into cubes. Combine green onions, garlic powder, parsley and sherry wine in plastic bag. Add venison to bag. Shake bag and store overnight in refrigerator. Start grill. Skewer venison and vegetables evenly. Grill on hot coals for 4 minutes on each side.

Jay Ramsey
Fresno, California

Dried Venison

Serves: varies
Prep Time: 4-5 hours

venison
Mexican salsa

Put meat in roasting pan, adding enough water to prevent burning. Roast at 300-350 degrees until meat pulls apart from bone. (Check regularly and add water if needed.) When meat can be pulled apart, shred it with 2 forks or fingers; the finer the better. Squeeze as much liquid out of meat as possible. Save broth. Put meat back in pan and cover with salsa. Simmer for about 1 hour. Hand-squeeze meat and save juice. Spread meat on cookie sheets. Air-dry or dry in warm oven. Put meat in freezer bags and freeze. Skim fat and salsa juice off top. Serve at room temperature as finger-food appetizer or microwave and serve with soft flour tortilla.

Dave Crowther
Bluemont, Virginia

Those Venison Things

Serves: 8-10
Prep Time: varies

10 venison slices, ½ inch wide; 4 inches long
¼ cup butter or olive oil
1 pkg. prepared crescent rolls
prepared mustard
fresh pepper to taste
10 cheddar or American cheese slices
1 egg
2 T. water or milk
sesame seeds (or poppy seeds)

Saute venison in olive oil for 5 minutes to par cook. Separate rolls. Brush each roll with prepared mustard. Season meat with pepper. Lay cheese slice on roll; add venison and roll up. Combine egg with water or milk to make egg wash. Brush meat with egg wash. Sprinkle sesame seeds on top. Using a well-greased cooking sheet, bake as directed on roll package. Serve in halves with drinks or soup. (For extra "zing," spread prepared horseradish on rolls before rolling up.)

Walter Squier
Portland, Connecticut

Roast Venison Backstrap

Serves: 4
Prep Time: 30 minutes

1 venison backstrap
salt and pepper to taste
aluminum foil

Preheat oven to 375 degrees. Season backstrap with salt and pepper and wrap in thick foil. Roast for about 30 minutes. (Do not overcook.) Meat should be pink in the middle. Remove and let cool. Serve with mustard or mayonnaise on crackers.

C.E. Kuempel
Pflugerville, Texas

Venison Mexicali Rose

Serves: 4
Prep Time: 45 minutes

- **1 lb. ground venison**
- **2 4-oz. cans whole green chilis**
- **1 lb. cheddar cheese, grated**
- **2 eggs**
- **½ cup flour**
- **1⅓ cups milk**
- **1 tsp. salt**

Brown venison and pour off any grease. Place layer of chilis on bottom of casserole dish and top with thin layer of meat. Add thin layer of cheese. Repeat layering process. Combine eggs, flour, milk and salt in separate bowl; blend. Pour mixture over top of layers. Bake (uncovered) at 350 degrees until a custard-like topping appears.

Mark Slack
Eureka, California

Wild Rice Dressing

Serves: 4-6
Prep Time 30-45 minutes

- **1 lb. ground venison**
- **1 lb. pork sausage**
- **1 cup celery, sliced or diced**
- **1 large can mushrooms**
- **1 cup wild rice, cooked**
- **your favorite spices**

Saute meat, adding celery and mushrooms when almost done. (Celery should be done, but crispy.) Add meat mixture to cooked wild rice. Season with your favorite spices.

Raymond Phillips Jr.
Escanaba, Michigan

Squier's Spanish Rice

Serves: 5-6
Prep Time: 45 minutes

½ lb. venison sausage
1 cup long grain rice
3-4 T. bacon drippings
1 red onion, chopped
⅓ cup green or red peppers, chopped
2 cups tomatoes
¼ cup Heinz 57 sauce
¾ tsp. salt
⅛ tsp. ground pepper
¼ cup parsley
2 T. lemon juice
dash of ground cinnamon
¼ tsp. garlic salt
2 cups water

Saute rice in bacon drippings until golden. Drain (saving drippings). Saute onion and pepper in drippings until onion is tender. Add remaining ingredients. Cover and simmer over low flame until all liquid is gone and rice is tender.

Walter Squier
Portland, Connecticut

Venison Egg Rolls

Serves: 60-80 egg rolls
Prep Time: 3-4 hours

2½ lbs. venison steak
½ cup flour
cooking oil
½ cup soy sauce
3 cabbage heads
6 carrots, shredded
½ lb. bean sprouts
1 can water chestnuts
2 small cans mushrooms
salt and pepper to taste
onion salt to taste
garlic powder to taste
80 egg roll wrappers

Cut meat into bite-sized pieces. Dredge meat in flour. Sir-fry meat in oil and soy sauce. (Set aside). Stir-fry remaining ingredients (except wrappers) until almost done. Add meat to vegetable mixture. Put ¼ cup mixture in each wrapper and roll according to directions on wrappers. Heat oil and deep-fry.

Mike Thompson
Oklahoma City, Oklahoma

Venison Sausage Strata

Serves: 4
Prep Time: overnight plus 2 hours

- 1/2 **lb. venison sausage, in casing or bulk**
- 1/2 **cup green bell peppers, chopped**
- 1/2 **cup yellow onion, chopped**
- 1 **16-oz. can tomatoes, drained**
- 8 **Italian or sandwich bread slices**
- 3 **eggs (4 if small)**
- 2 1/2 **cups whole milk**
- 1 **tsp. salt**
- 1/8 **tsp. pepper**
- 1/4 **tsp. oregano**
- 1/8 **tsp. basil**
- 2 **T. fresh Parmesan cheese, grated**

Remove casings and brown sausage in large frying pan. (Cook about 8-10 minutes, breaking up meat.) Add peppers, and onion. Cook for 5 minutes. Add drained tomatoes, breaking them up. Cook for 10-15 minutes to remove most liquid. Lay 4 bread slices in 8x8-inch pan. Spread meat mixture over bread. Add remaining bread slices over meat. Beat eggs, milk and spices. Slowly pour spice mixture over bread. Sprinkle cheese on top. Cover with plastic wrap and refrigerate overnight. Bake strata at 325 degrees for about 1 hour or until puffy and golden brown. Let stand 5-7 minutes before serving.

Walter Squier
Portland, Connecticut

Red's Venison Soup

Serves 3-4
Prep Time: 2 hours

2-3 lbs. venison	**¹⁄₄ tsp. garlic salt**
4 cups water	**1 tsp. black pepper**
¹⁄₂ large onion, chopped	**¹⁄₂ tsp. seasoning salt**
3-4 medium potatoes, cubed	**2 cans whole tomatoes**
	1 can kernel corn
1 tsp. salt	

Cook meat in water for about 1 hour. Add onion, potatoes and
half of seasonings. Cook for 30 minutes. Add tomatoes, corn
and remaining seasonings. Cook for another 30 minutes.

Beryl Lockett
Oak Hill, West Virginia

Game Heart

Serves: 4-5
Prep Time: overnight plus 5-8 minutes

1 venison heart
1 cup red wine
2 T. vinegar
1 tsp. salt
2 peppercorns
1 tsp. prepared mustard
1 medium onion, sliced
1 bay leaf
flour
2 T. butter

Split heart in half (top to bottom) and remove all vents and
ducts. Soak halves in marinade of wine, vinegar, salt,
peppercorns, mustard, onion and bay leaf overnight. After
marinating, roll heart in flour and fry in butter. Sear thoroughly.
Reduce heat slightly and cook for about 5 minutes.

Jerry Marshall
Beavercreek, Oregon

Stuffed Venison Heart With Brandy Gravy

Serves: 2
Prep Time: overnight plus 2 hours

1 **venison heart**	⅛ **tsp. ground sage**
1 **T. salt**	**salt and pepper to taste**
1 **qt. water**	1 **tsp. butter**
¼ **cup bread crumbs**	**milk**
¼ **cup celery, chopped**	½ **cup beef broth**
¼ **cup onion, chopped**	¼ **cup brandy**

Combine salt and water for marinade. Place heart in marinade overnight. When ready to cook, preheat oven to 350 degrees. Mix bread crumbs, celery, onion, sage, butter and salt and pepper with a little milk to bind and moisten stuffing. Stuff heart, then close with skewers. Put heart into pan and pour in broth and brandy. Cover pan and bake for 2 hours.

Thomas Long Jr.
Mill Hall, Pennsylvania

Deer Hearts

Serves: 3-5
Prep Time: 1 hour

4 **deer hearts**	2 **cans red roasted**
olive oil	**peppers, chopped**
2 **T. garlic, minced**	3 **T. hot cherry peppers**
2 **onions, minced**	1 **T. parsley**
1 **28-oz. can tomato sauce**	1 **T. oregano**
1 **28-oz. can tomatoes**	

Boil deer hearts until they change color (about 5 minutes), then cut into small pieces. Brown hearts in olive oil with 1 T. garlic. Brown onions in olive oil, adding remaining garlic. After hearts and onions are done, combine in pot. Add remaining ingredients. Bring to a boil. Simmer for 30 minutes. Serve over spaghetti.

Robert Brienza
Scotia, New York

Perfect Deer Liver

Serves: 2-4
Prep Time: 20-30 minutes

2 lbs. deer liver	2 eggs
1/2 cup onion, finely chopped	1/2 cup water
2 cups bread crumbs	4 T. butter
2 tsp. salt	2 T. oil
1/2 tsp. pepper	

Mix together onion, bread crumbs, salt and pepper. Combine egg and water and beat with fork. Place deer liver in egg, then bread crumbs. Set aside. Heat butter and oil. Place liver in crumb mixture again, then in hot skillet. Cook on medium-high setting until done. (Do not overcook.) Slice liver about 1/4 inch thick for best results.

Eric Helstrom
Plainfield, Connecticut

Venison Michigan Sauce

Serves: 2-4
Prep Time: 45 minutes

1 lb. ground venison	1 T. brown sugar
1 medium onion, finely chopped	1/2 tsp. red cayenne pepper
1 small green pepper, finely chopped	1/2 tsp. oregano
1 small can tomato sauce	1/2 tsp. garlic salt
1 cup catsup	

Brown meat, onion and green pepper in oil. Add remaining ingredients and simmer for 30 minutes. Serve on hotdogs or use as gravy on meatloaf or potatoes.

Robert Brienza
Scotia, New York

Venison Steak And Onion Pie

Serves: 3-5
Prep Time: 2 hours

1 **lb. venison steak,
   cubed**
1 **cup onions, sliced**
¼ **cup shortening**
¼ **cup flour**
½ **tsp. salt**
½ **tsp. pepper**
½ **tsp. paprika**
2½ **cups boiling water**
2 **cups potatoes, diced
   pastry for 1 crust**

Pastry:
2¼ **cups flour**
½ **tsp. salt**
⅔ **cup shortening**
⅓ **cup water**

Cook onions slowly in melted shortening. Remove onions. Roll
meat in mixture of flour and seasonings. Brown meat in
shortening. Add boiling water, cover and simmer for 1 hour.
Add potatoes and cook 10 minutes longer. Pour in greased
casserole dish, then cover with cooked onions. Place crust,
rolled ¼ inch thick, on top. Bake at 400 degrees for 30-35
minutes.

For pastry: Combine flour and salt in mixing bowl. Cut
shortening into flour with pastry blender or 2 knives. Do not
over mix. Add water gradually, sprinkling 1 T. at a time over
mixture. Toss lightly with fork until flour particles have
dampened. Roll on flour covered surface.

John Keister
Mifflinburg, Pennsylvania

Poncho's Mexican Meat Pie

Serves: 3-5
Prep Time: 1 hour, 15 minutes

1½ **lbs. ground venison**
½ **lb. hot Italian sausage**
3 **beef bouillon cubes**
1¼ **cups hot water**
3 **garlic cloves, minced**
¼ **cup green chilis,**
  chopped
½ **tsp. ground mace**
¾ **tsp. ground pepper**
¼ **tsp. celery seed**
¼ **tsp. cloves, ground**
½ **cup yellow onions,**
  chopped
¼ **cup tomato juice**
3 **T. cornstarch**
  salt and pepper to taste
1 **cup Monterey Jack**
  cheese, shredded
1 **pastry crust**

Saute meat, removing sausage from casings. Dissolve bouillon cube in hot water. Add garlic, chilis, bouillon, spices and onions. Blend tomato juice and cornstarch, stirring in slowly. Turn up heat and bring to boil. Lower flame and simmer (covered) for 10 minutes. Season with salt and pepper. Pour into prepared crust. Add half of cheese, top crust, then remaining cheese. Bake at 425 degrees for 30 minutes. Serve with green salad.

Walter Squier
Portland, Connecticut

Venison Pot Pie

Serves: 6
Prep Time: 2 hours

**2 cups venison, cooked
and cubed
3 T. butter
3 T. flour
1 tsp. salt
1/4 tsp. pepper
1/2 tsp. marjoram,
crushed
1/2 tsp. thyme, crushed
1 cup stock (game, beef
or chicken)
1/4 cup onion, chopped
1/4 cup celery, chopped
1 10-oz. pkg. frozen
mixed vegetables
1 medium potato, cubed
and cooked
pastry for 9-inch, 2-
crust pie
1/2 cup half & half cream**

Melt butter in large pan over low heat. Stir in flour, salt, pepper and herbs. Cook, stirring until mixture is smooth and bubbly. Add stock, stirring constantly. Cook for 1 minute, then stir in meat and vegetables. Remove from heat and add cream. Pour filling into pastry-lined pan. Arrange top crust and flute edges. Bake 35-40 minutes at 425 degrees. If crust starts browning too fast, cover with aluminum foil.

Chuck Little
Fairview, Montana

Deer Pot Pie

Serves: 6-8
Prep Time: 2 hours

2-3 lbs. venison, cut into bite-sized pieces	**1 cup stock**
1 onion, quartered	**1 cup milk**
4 T. butter or margarine	**salt to taste**
4 T. flour	**1 1-oz. can sliced carrots**
6 T. Sauer's brown gravy mix	**1 1-oz. can potatoes**
	1 pie crust

Place onion and bay leaf in bottom of pressure cooker. Add vegetables, meat and water; cook under 15 lbs. of pressure for 20 minutes. Cool cooker immediately. Strain stock and reserve for use in sauce. Place meat and vegetables in casserole dish. In medium saucepan, melt butter and blend in flour and gravy mix. Stir in stock, milk and salt. Pour into casserole dish. Make slits in pie crust and cover casserole. Bake at 425 degrees for 25-30 minutes or until crust is browned and sauce is bubbly.

Joe Heatwole
Harrisonburg, Virginia

Venison And Tomato Bake

Serves: 2-4
Prep Time: 1 hour, 15 minutes

3-4 lbs. venison	**$1/2$ T. oregano**
1 qt. whole tomatoes and sauce	**$1/2$ tsp. garlic**
$3/4$ cup onions, chopped	**salt and pepper to taste**

Brown meat in baking pan. Mix remaining ingredients together and pour over meat. Cook for 1 hour, basting until meat is done. Add water if needed. Serve with boiled potatoes and carrots.

Sherry Elson
Lansford, North Dakota

Southern Cooking

Southern Wild Game Cooking

by Wayne and Sherry Fears

Mention Southern game cooking and most people will see images of country-fried venison steak with gravy, fried okra, blackeyed peas and corn bread. While fried foods, dried beans and corn bread are traditional Southern dishes, there's much more to the region's fare than that. The food of the South is as varied as its people. And, game has always been a significant part of the Southern menu—partly out of necessity and partly from the desire to enjoy the goodness of nature's bounty.

The first European adventurers in the South learned to harvest and prepare wild foods from the Shawnee, Cherokee, Creek, Choctaw, Chickasaw and Seminole Indians. Mixed with this Native American fare were culinary techniques from Spanish explorers, French and English traders, Scotch-Irish longhunters, German settlers and African slaves. Each added the best of their traditional meal preparation to create the basis of what is now known as "Southern Cooking."

The early South was a land of sharp contrasts, and its menus reflected these differences. Simple menus relying heavily on game and wild plants were most often the table fare for settlers in the remote coves of the southern Appalachians, trappers living along the creeks and river drainages, sharecroppers living on small patch farms and slaves living in cabins behind "the big house."

Often the entire kitchen for these people consisted of a cast-iron Dutch oven and cast-iron skillet. The cooking was done in the cabin fireplace. Living off the land was more than a trendy phrase; it was a necessary skill. If you didn't catch it, kill it or pick it, you didn't eat it. The lady of the house was challenged to take a rabbit or two, some freshly-picked young pokeweed, or "poke sallit," a little cornmeal and the roots of a sassafras tree and create a filling meal for a hungry husband and a houseful of growing youngsters.

In contrast, the large farms and plantations had large kitchens with plenty of helping hands for preparing wild boar barbecue, batter-fried venison steaks, quail with wine and wild turkey and dressing. There were plenty of dried beans and fresh vegetables from the large gardens and, also, an abundance of flour and cornmeal from the local grist mill.

Having wild game dinners with all the trimmings was a common form of entertainment associated with quail hunts, fox hunts, horse races, weddings and social gatherings. Hunting for meat, the profitable deer hide market and the clearing of large tracts of land for cotton plantations took their toll on the big-game population of the South, however. By the time of the Civil War, the region had seriously reduced its whitetail deer and wild turkey populations.

Following the Civil War, the Southern landscape was transfigured by displaced city dwellers, freed slaves, deposed plantation owners and carpetbaggers. By the turn of the century, the South was dotted with small patch farms into which many of the large plantations had been divided. Though there were few deer and turkeys, patch farming provided the perfect habitat for flourishing small-game populations. The differences in lifestyles and financial status were not so great as they had been, and through the convergence of contrasting lifestyles, what is now thought of as traditional Southern Cooking survived.

This land experienced further changes in the twentieth century that affected its wildlife populations and people's eating habits. Restocking deer and turkeys began in the 1940s. Establishing hunting seasons and more sophisticated wildlife law enforcement protected game. Industrialization and new land management practices, including forest products industries, meant fewer small farms and more big-game habitat.

Today, the South has cities and small towns, farms and industry, forests and fields. It is, in a word, diverse. True to their reputation, many Southerners still love fried foods such as fried venison steak, fried squirrel, fried quail, fried okra, fried green tomatoes, fried squash, fried eggplant and fried apple pies. But, like the rest of the country, Southerners know that frying isn't the most healthful way to prepare food. What was once fried in animal fat is now cooked in vegetable oil, and foods are more likely to be baked, broiled, grilled, barbecued or boiled. "Seasoning" now means more than salt, pepper and fatback to most Southerners.

Southerners still remain proud of their culinary heritage and enjoy introducing curious "foreigners" to traditional foods. When Stagshead hunting lodge in Alabama opened, most hunters were businessmen from the big cities of the North. The lodge planned meals that it thought they'd be familiar with: large New York strip steaks, fresh garden salads, baked potatoes (with a variety of toppings) and cheesecake. One by one the Northern guests said they were hoping to sample some traditional Southern Cooking. They said they could have steaks any time.

You should have heard the singing from the local ladies who worked in the lodge kitchen when the menu was changed to chicken-fried steak with gravy, boiled cabbage, sweet potatoes, turnip greens, field peas, corn bread and blackberry cobbler. From then on, the Northern guests came to eat more than to hunt. Traditional Southern meals were a winner. The lodge guests were often caught sneaking into the kitchen to get recipes from the cooks.

Wild game dinners are as much a part of heritage as the hunt that produces the game. There's nothing more satisfying than preparing for the hunt, harvesting an animal in a fair chase and offering the land's bounty to your family in a traditional meal.

The following recipes consist of a variety of game and non-game dishes. Many are generations old. (Some date to the late 1700s.) They were created for people who worked long, hard hours, enjoyed hunting and enjoyed eating the bounty of the land. Those grouped together are traditional Southern meals you would likely find on a table South of the Mason Dixon line in 1793 or 1993. Enjoy them all.

Stuffed 'Possum And Sweet 'Taters Dinner

When it comes to "unusual" game that is enjoyed on the Southern table, 'possum tops the list. Here's a dinner that might put this homely critter at the top of your list, too.

Stuffed 'Possum

Serves: 5
Prep Time: 3 hours

1 2¹/₂-lb. opossum	¹/₃ cup flour
salt	2 T. brown sugar
pepper	
sage	
butter or margarine	
3-4 sweet potatoes	

Prepare stuffing (below). Rub inside of dressed opossum with seasonings. Loosely fill opossum with stuffing. Truss, season and place opossum on greased rack in shallow pan. If lean, brush with butter and cover loosely with aluminum foil. Roast (uncovered) at 300-325 degrees for 1-2 hours, about 30-35 minutes per pound. During last 30 minutes, remove foil and place parboiled sweet potatoes (peeled and halved) around opossum. Baste meat and potatoes several times with drippings in pan. (Dust meat with flour and potatoes with brown sugar after each basting.) Place potatoes around opossum on heated platter, garnish and serve.

Apple And Raisin Stuffing

6 cups bread cubes	1¹/₄ tsp. poultry seasoning
1 tsp. salt	¹/₃ cup water
¹/₄ cup apple, diced	
pepper to taste	
¹/₄ cup raisins	

Combine dry ingredients. Add water and mix thoroughly.

Southern
New Year's Dinner

This traditional, complete Southern dinner is often served on New Year's Day. Though it won't cure a hangover, it is believed to bring good luck throughout the new year. While the traditional main dish would be made with domestic hog jowl, hunters substitute a wild boar ham hock for equally delicious results.

Wild boar meat can be tasty, or it can be so strong and gamey that dogs won't eat it. Fitness for the table relies on a number of things including the hog's age, regular diet, the time of year and other uncontrollable factors. However, proper field care, particularly in the warm Southern U.S., is of utmost importance. For the most delicious eating, shoot a small to mid-sized hog and dress it out immediately. Move it to a cooler and get the hide off as quickly as possible.

Ham Hock And Black-Eyed Peas

Serves: 4
Prep Time: 3 hours

1 small ham hock
2 cups dried black-eyed
** peas**
8 cups cold water
1 cup rice, uncooked
** salt and pepper to taste**

Soak dried peas in cold water for 3-4 hours. Add ham hock and bring to a boil. Cover and reduce heat, continuing to simmer for 2 hours. Add rice and simmer for 45 minutes or until rice and peas are done and liquid is almost absorbed. Remove meat from bone. Season with salt and pepper. Serve peas and rice on hot platter with ham on top.

(Southern New Year's Dinner Cont'd)

Sassafras Tea

Serves: 4
Prep Time: 15 minutes

**26 sassafras tree roots, 3
      inches long
      water
      sugar to taste**

Boil sassafras tree roots in water until a pale reddish color is
achieved. Sweeten with sugar and serve hot.

Southern Spoonbread

Serves: 4
Prep Time: 45 minutes

**2 cups milk
1 cup water
1 cup yellow cornmeal
2 T. margarine
1 tsp. salt
3 eggs**

Combine ingredients (except eggs) and cook over medium
heat until thickened, stirring constantly. Remove from heat. Beat
eggs until thick. Gradually stir about 1/4 of hot mixture into eggs;
add to remaining hot mixture, stirring constantly. Pour into
lightly greased 1 1/2 qt. casserole dish. Bake at 350 degrees for
35 minutes.

Fried Woodchuck And Turnip Greens Dinner

This complete Southern dinner is a direct reflection of the Southerner's desire to use all his game wisely. A woodchuck needs to be removed from the pasture. Why not utilize the delicious meat to its fullest? Although Northerners might relish the turnip root, the Southerner knows the greens on top are even better. "Waste not want not" is a traditional theme in most types of Southern cooking.

"Greens" of all sorts are staples in traditional Southern cooking. Some of the more common ones you'll hear about are collard greens, and turnip greens. For lack of a better comparison, the use of greens is similar to that of Swiss chard or spinach. Greens are quite high in fiber, and a healthful part of the Southern diet.

The baked bean recipe here is just one example of the wide use of a variety of beans in traditional Southern cooking.

The "finishing touch" to this meal is added by including Southern Biscuits as prepared for the Venison Liver Dinner on page 95.

Southern-Fried Woodchuck

Serves: 4-6
Prep Time: 2 hours

- **1 woodchuck**
- **1 T. salt**
- **water**
- **1 cup flour**
- **vegetable oil**

Clean woodchuck and cut into 6-7 pieces. Parboil in salted water for 1 hour. Remove from broth, roll in flour and fry in hot oil until brown.

(Fried Woodchuck And Turnip Greens Dinner Cont'd)

Turnip Greens

Serves: 4-6
Prep Time: 1 hour, 15 minutes

- **2 lbs. fresh turnip greens**
- **6 bacon slices, chopped**
- **4 cups water**
- **1 T. sugar**
- **1/2 tsp. salt**

Wash greens and drain. Tear into bite-sized pieces. Cook bacon in Dutch oven until brown. Drain bacon and set aside. Keep drippings in Dutch oven. Add greens and water. Stir in sugar and salt. Cover and cook for 40 minutes. Spoon into serving dish, and sprinkle crumbled bacon on top.

Southern Baked Beans

Serves: 4-6
Prep Time: 12 hours

- **2 cups dried pinto beans**
- **water**
- **1/2 tsp. salt**
- **1/2 salt pork, cubed**
- **1/2 cup onion, chopped**
- **1/2 cup molasses**
- **2 T. catsup**
- **1/2 tsp. prepared mustard**
- **1/4 tsp. pepper**
- **2 cups hot water**

Sort and wash beans; place in large Dutch oven. Cover with water 2 inches above beans; let soak for 8 hours. Drain. Cover beans with water and add salt; bring to a boil. Cover, reduce heat and simmer for 2 hours. Drain. Place beans in greased 2½-qt. baking dish. Add salt pork and onion. Combine remaining ingredients and pour over beans. Cover and bake at 350 degrees for 2 hours, stirring once.

Venison Pot Roast Dinner With Hoe Cake Or Pan Bread

This is a Southern dinner that goes way, way back. There were Southerners who were so poor, they owned only a few cooking utensils. The pot roast-style dinner made efficient use of the single pot that the household owned by preparing meat and vegetables in it at one time.

Pan bread is another traditional Southern favorite which compliments the delicious venison pot roast dinner. There's nothing better than pan bread for soppin' up every last drop of delicious juice from your plate. This bread will leave the plate so clean, the hounds won't take the time to lick it!

Venison Pot Roast Dinner

Serves: 6-8
Prep Time: 4 hours

    1 4-lb. venison roast (use cuts
       from the chuck, round or rump)
  1/4 cup salt pork or bacon, cubed
    3 T. butter or drippings
 1 1/2 cups hot water
    1 cup tart fruit juice or cider
    1 celery stalk, sliced
    1 tsp. parsley flakes
  1/4 tsp. thyme
    1 tsp. salt
  1/4 tsp. pepper
    6 potatoes, peeled and quartered
    6 carrots, peeled and quartered
    6 onions, chopped
  2-3 T. flour

Insert cubes of salt pork into small cuts in roast. Heat butter in Dutch oven or deep casserole and brown meat on all sides. Add hot water, fruit juice, celery, parsley, thyme, salt and pepper. Cover and simmer gently for 3 hours on top of stove or in oven at 350 degrees until tender. If liquid gets too low, add water. About 1 hour before meal is ready, add potatoes, carrots and onions. Add a little additional salt for vegetables. When

(Venison Pot Roast Dinner With Hoe Cake Or Pan Bread Cont'd)

vegetables are tender, put meat and vegetables on platter and keep hot. Thicken liquid with flour. Serve gravy hot with roast and vegetables.

Tater Knob Hoe Cake

Serves: 6-8
Prep Time: 15 minutes

- **2 cups self-rising corn-meal**
- **salt**
- **2 eggs**
- **buttermilk**

Heat cast-iron skillet with just enough vegetable oil to cover bottom lightly. Mix cornmeal, salt, eggs and water or buttermilk into thick paste. Pour enough paste into skillet for 6-inch cake. Brown on bottom and turn. Remove from skillet when both sides are golden brown.

Pan Bread

Serves: 5
Prep Time: 25 minutes

- **1 cup flour**
- **1/4 tsp. salt**
- **2 T. powdered skim milk**
- **1 tsp. double-action baking powder**

Grease cast-iron skillet and heat. Add enough cold water to ingredients to make soft dough. Mold into cake, about 1 inch thick, and lay in hot skillet. Cook on medium heat until crust forms on bottom, then turn over and form crust on other side. Reduce heat to low and cook for 15 minutes or until golden brown.

Venison Liver Dinner With Hominy Casserole

Venison liver has taken a bad rap lately. Nutritionists tell us it is high in cholesterol and that the liver is where chemicals like pesticides and heavy metals are likely to build up in a deer's system. There's probably no denying that, but few Southern hunters can pass up a traditional deer camp meal of fresh venison liver, especially when it's prepared with a down home favorite like hominy casserole.

And, besides, how bad can it be if you enjoy venison liver only once a year? If we all believed everything the papers told us, nobody would eat a nice juicy hamburger either!

This complete meal is best rounded out with turnip greens prepared like those for the Woodchuck and Turnip Greens recipe from page 90.

Venison Liver With Onions In Olive Oil

Serves: 4
Prep Time: 45 minutes

> 1 **venison liver, thinly sliced**
> **water**
> 1 **large onion, sliced**
> 1¼ **T. olive oil**
> 1 **T. butter**
> **salt and pepper to taste**
> **lemon juice**

Slice liver thin. Cover with water and bring to a boil. Remove liver from water. Saute onion in olive oil and butter. Add liver and continue frying until liver is done. (Liver will be tough if overcooked.) Season meat with salt and pepper, then drizzle with lemon juice.

(Venison Liver Dinner With Hominy Casserole Cont'd)

Hominy Casserole

Serves: 4
Prep Time: 40 minutes

- **½ cup onion, chopped**
- **2 T. margarine**
- **3 cans golden hominy, drained**
- **2 4-oz. cans chopped green chilis, drained**
- **2 cups cheddar cheese, shredded**

In large skillet, saute onion in margarine for 5 minutes. Add hominy, chilis and 1 cup cheese. Mix well. Pour into lightly greased 10x6x2-inch baking dish. Bake at 400 degrees for 20 minutes. Sprinkle remaining 1 cup cheese over top. Bake for 5 more minutes. Serve with turnip greens and biscuits.

Biscuits

Serves: 4-6
Prep Time: 30 minutes

- **2 cups flour**
- **2 tsp. sugar**
- **5 tsp. baking soda**
- **½ tsp. salt**
- **¼ cup shortening**
- **1¼ cups buttermilk**

Mix first 4 ingredients and stir. Add shortening and mix well until mixture is consistency of meal. Stir in buttermilk. Roll dough ½ inch thick. Cut into 3-inch biscuits. Place in greased pan about ½ inch apart. Bake for 10-12 minutes until golden brown.

Crockpot Rabbit

Serves: 6-8
Prep Time: 5 hours

2-3 rabbits

Barbecue sauce:

1 cup onion, diced	**3 T. Worcestershire**
¼ cup oil	**sauce**
¼ cup lemon juice	**½ tsp. pepper**
¼ cup brown sugar	**1 T. salt**
3 T. mustard	**1 8-oz. can tomato sauce**
3 T. vinegar	

Place rabbit sections into Crockpot. Prepare barbecue sauce: Pan-fry onions in oil until tender. Add remaining ingredients and cook 20 minutes over low heat. Then, add barbecue sauce to Crockpot, covering rabbits. Cook on high for 4 hours or on low for 8 hours.

Squirrel And Dumplings

Serves: 6-8
Prep Time: 1 hour

3 squirrels	**Dumplings:**
salt	**3 cups flour**
3 qts. water	**6 T. shortening**
1 cup sweet milk	**milk**
2 T. butter	
pepper to taste	

Boil squirrels in salted water until tender. Take out squirrels and let cool. Prepare dumplings: Mix flour and shortening together until mixture looks like meal. Add enough milk to make stiff dough. Knead well, dusting with flour, and roll thin. Cut into strips; set aside. Add sweet milk and butter to broth. Heat broth to boiling. Drop dumplings into boiling broth. While dumplings are cooking, remove squirrel meat from bone and add to dumplings. Season with pepper when dumplings are done (about 15 minutes).

Squirrel Brunswick Stew

Serves: 6-8
Prep Time: 3 hours, 30 minutes

2 **squirrels**	6 **potatoes**
1 **T. salt**	1 **tsp. pepper**
4 **qts. water**	2 **tsp. sugar**
1 **onion, minced**	1 **qt. stewed tomatoes**
1 **pt. lima beans**	1/2 **lb. butter**
6 **corn ears**	**water**
1/2 **lb. salt pork**	

Cut squirrel into pieces. Add salt to water and bring to a boil. Then, add onion, beans, corn, pork, potatoes, pepper and squirrels. Cover tightly and simmer for 2 hours. Remove squirrel pieces and bone. Return meat to stew. Add sugar and tomatoes and simmer for 1 hour. Ten minutes before removing stew from fire, add butter. Add salt and pepper, if needed, and pour into a tureen. Serve in soup bowls.

Sherried Quail

Serves: 2-4
Prep Time: 1 hour, 15 minutes

> **4 whole quail**
> **salt and pepper to taste**
> **1/2 cup butter or**
> **margarine**
> **1 cup sherry**

Thoroughly clean each bird. Season birds with salt and pepper; and brown evenly in butter. Pour sherry over them and cover. Simmer in skillet for 45 minutes or until tender.

Roasted Quail With Mushrooms

Serves: 4
Prep Time: 1 hour

> **4 quail**
> **4 bacon slices**
> **1 T. butter or margarine**
> **1/2 cup hot water**
> **juice of 1/2 lemon**
> **1 3-oz. can broiled**
> **mushrooms, drained**

Clean quail inside and out. Bind each bird with bacon slice, securing with toothpick. Put birds into greased pan and roast at 350 degrees, basting occasionally, for about 30 minutes or until tender. Remove birds and add butter, water and lemon juice to drippings in pan, stirring to make gravy. Add mushrooms. Serve birds with gravy.

Fried Quail

Serves: 4
Prep Time: 30 minutes

> **4 quail**
> **1/4 cup flour**
> **1 tsp. salt**
> **1/2 tsp. pepper**
> **vegetable oil**

Dredge quail with mixture of flour, salt and pepper. Have frying pan half-filled with hot oil. Brown quail on both sides. Reduce heat and cover skillet. Cook slowly until tender, about 20 minutes, turning once to brown evenly.

Smoked Wild Turkey

Serves: 8
Prep Time: 8 hours, 15 minutes

> **1 turkey, dressed with**
> **skin**
> **1 1/2 cups dry white wine**
> **water**
> **1 bay leaf, crushed**
> **1/4 tsp. tarragon leaves**
> **1 tsp. parsley, minced**
> **seasoned salt**

Place turkey in enameled pan with white wine and water to cover. Add bay leaf, tarragon and parsley to marinade. Cover and place in refrigerator overnight. Remove turkey from marinade and pat dry with paper towels. Sprinkle with seasoned salt. Place marinade in smoker's water pan, adding more water if necessary. Place turkey on oiled rack and cover smoker. Cook for 6-8 hours.

Roasted Wild Turkey & Corn Bread Dressing

Serves: 8-10
Prep Time: 4-6 hours

1 9-lb. turkey
salt and pepper
butter

Dressing:
- **6 bread slices, lightly toasted and cubed**
- **6 cups corn bread (without crust)**
- **1/4 tsp. pepper**
- **2-3 tsp. sage**
- **1 tsp. salt**
- **1 1/2 cups onions, chopped**
- **1/2 cup celery, finely chopped (optional)**
- **1/2 cup walnuts, chopped**
- **1/4 cup butter or margarine**
- **1/4 cup water**
- **3 eggs, lightly beaten (optional)**

Remove turkey wings and set aside for dressing. Season turkey (inside and out) with salt and pepper. Rub with butter. Place turkey (breast up) on rack on roasting pan. To prevent drying, cover bird with aluminum foil tent. Roast at 325 degrees, for 20-25 minutes per pound or until tender, basting frequently with pan drippings. Meanwhile, boil wings in water until meat comes off bone easily. Set aside broth and bone wings. For dressing: Combine bread and other dry ingredients. Add butter to water, then gradually add to mixture, making sure ingredients are thoroughly soaked. Add lightly beaten eggs and mix well; then, add meat and mix again. Pour mixture into deep casserole. Bake at 375 degrees for 30-40 minutes or until dressing is lightly browned on top.

Baked Rattlesnake

Serves: 4
Prep Time: 1 hour, 15 minutes

- **1 rattlesnake**
- **1 tsp. basil**
- **1 can cream sauce**
- **1 tsp. white pepper**
- **1 jar sliced mushrooms**
- **1 tsp. rosemary**
- **2 limes, thinly sliced**

Skin, dress and wash snake in cold water. Cut into 3-inch pieces and place in large baking dish. Cover with cream sauce and add mushrooms, limes, basil, pepper and rosemary. Cover tightly. Bake at 300 degrees for 1 hour or until done.

Marinated Doves

Serves: 5-6
Prep Time: 1 hour

- **12 doves**
- **1/2 stick butter, melted**
- **juice of 1/2 lemon**
- **1 cup sherry, extra-dry**
- **1/4 cup cooking oil**

Combine butter, lemon juice, sherry and oil. Pour mixture over doves. Marinate doves for 5-6 hours or overnight. Bake (uncovered) at 350 degrees for 30-40 minutes, basting frequently. Birds should be slightly pink and juicy. (Do not overcook.)

Wood Duck With Pecan Stuffing

Serves: 4
Prep Time: 1 hour, 30 minutes

4 wood ducks
4 cups bread crumbs
1 cup celery, finely chopped
1 cup onion, finely chopped
1 cup raisins (seedless)
1 cup pecans, chopped
1/2 tsp. salt
1/2 cup milk, scalded
2 eggs, beaten
12 bacon slices
1 cup catsup
1/4 cup Worcestershire sauce
1/4 cup A-1 sauce
1/2 cup chili sauce

Mix bread crumbs, celery, onion, raisins, pecans and salt together. Add hot milk to beaten eggs and then add to dry mixture. Loosely fill ducks with this stuffing. Place in roaster and cover duck with bacon strips. Roast (uncovered) at 350 degrees, 20 minutes per pound. About 20 minutes before serving, combine catsup, Worcestershire sauce, A-1 sauce and chili sauce and baste ducks. Skim fat from sauce and serve sauce with ducks.

Beaver Atlanta Special

Serves: 8
Prep Time: 10 hours

1 **beaver**	1-2 **garlic cloves, chopped**
water	**celery leaves (optional)**
salt	**flour**
1 **bay leaf**	**vegetable oil**
2 **medium onions,**	**salt and pepper to taste**
chopped	

Remove nearly all fat from beaver and cut into sections. Soak meat overnight in saltwater. Parboil meat in water with bay leaves, onions and garlic until half-cooked. (Celery may be added, if desired.) Drain meat, roll in flour and brown in hot oil. Season with salt and pepper. Bake (covered) in moderate oven until tender. Gravy can be made from drippings.

Venison Ka-Bobs

Serves: 4
Prep Time: 1 hour, 30 minutes

- **2 lbs. venison loin or rump**
- **1 pkg. meat marinade**
- **3-4 large onions, cut into 12 sections**
- **2 bell peppers, each cut into 8 pieces**
- **1 lb. mushrooms**
- **12 cherry tomatoes or 3 quartered tomatoes**
- **1 large bottle Italian dressing**

Cut meat into 1-inch cubes. Mix marinade according to package instructions and put into bowl with meat cubes. Put vegetables into bowl and cover with Italian dressing. Let vegetables and meat marinate for 4-6 hours. Put meat and vegetables alternately on skewers. Cook over grill or in broiler, rotating until lightly brown on each side. Serve with rice.

Apple Venison Balls

Serves: 4-5
Prep Time: 1 hour, 30 minutes

- **1 lb. ground venison**
- **1½ tsp. salt**
- **1 cup dry bread crumbs**
- **½ tsp. pepper**
- **1 cup fresh apple, grated**
- **2 eggs, beaten**
- **2 cups tomato juice**
- **2 tsp. sugar**

Combine all ingredients (except tomato juice and sugar) and mix thoroughly. Form mixture into balls. Place balls in 2-qt. casserole dish. Combine tomato juice and sugar, then pour over balls. Cover and bake at 350 degrees for 1 hour.

Southern Barbecued Venison Ribs

Serves: 4-6
Prep time: 4 hours

3 lbs. venison ribs

Sauce:
- **1 cup onion, finely chopped**
- **2 T. brown sugar**
- **1/2 cup celery, diced**
- **1/4 cup lemon juice**
- **1/2 cup vinegar cayenne pepper**
- **1/4 cup Worcestershire sauce**
- **2 T. butter**
- **2 cups catsup**
- **1 tsp. dry mustard**
- **1 T. molasses**
- **1/4 tsp. chili powder**
- **2 cups water**

Cut venison ribs into serving-size pieces and par boil. In separate pot, bring water to a boil. Then, add sauce ingredients and return to a boil. Reduce heat and simmer (for 5 minutes), stirring constantly. Place rib pieces in Dutch oven and pour sauce over ribs. Bake in slow oven (275 degrees) for 2-3 hours.

Baked Venison Heart

Serves: 4
Prep time: 1 hour

**1 venison heart, valves
and arteries removed**

Dressing:

1 large onion, diced	**1/2 loaf dry bread, cubed**
1 cup celery, finely	**1 tsp. salt**
chopped	**1/8 tsp. pepper**
1/2 cup butter	**1 tsp. sage**

Boil heart until tender. Prepare dressing: Cover onion and celery with a little water and simmer until tender. Add butter, heating until melted. Mix bread cubes, salt, pepper and sage. Pour liquid over bread and stir until moist. Split heart open and fill with dressing. Place remaining dressing around heart to completely cover. Bake about 30 minutes at 300 degrees or until dressing is lightly browned.

Southern Venison Stroganoff

Serves: 4
Prep Time: 2 hours

1 1/2 lbs. venison, cubed	**1/4 tsp. pepper**
1/2 cup onion, chopped	**1/4 tsp. paprika**
1/2 cup celery, chopped	**1 lb. fresh mushrooms**
1/4 cup butter	**1 can cream of chicken**
1 garlic clove, minced	**soup, condensed**
2 T. flour (optional)	**1 cup sour cream**
2 tsp. salt	**parsley, chives or dill**

In frying pan, saute onion and celery in melted butter until soft, but not brown. Stir in venison cubes, garlic, flour, salt, pepper, paprika and mushrooms. Saute mixture for 5 minutes. Add soup. Simmer (uncovered) for 20 minutes. Stir in sour cream and sprinkle with parsley, chives or dill. Thin with water as desired. Cover and simmer for about 1 hour. Serve on rice.

Buttermilk-Dipped Venison Fingers

Serves: 6-8
Prep Time: 30 minutes

1-2 **lbs. venison loin**
   flour
   salt and pepper to taste
1 **cup buttermilk**
1/2 **cup oil**

Cut meat into "fingers" (1/2 inch wide), cutting across the grain. Mix flour and salt and pepper in paper bag. Dip venison strips in buttermilk. Place dipped venison, one piece at a time, into bag and shake until covered with flour. Place in preheated oil over medium heat and fry until light golden brown.

Venison In Beer

Serves: 6-8
Prep Time: 3 hours

4 **lbs. venison, cubed**	3 **bay leaves**
vegetable oil	**parsley**
6 **cups onion, sliced**	1-2 **bottles of beer**
salt and pepper to taste	1-2 **T. cornstarch**
4 **garlic cloves, crushed**	1-2 **T. wine vinegar**
1 **can beef broth**	
3 **T. brown sugar**	
1/2 **tsp. thyme**	

Brown meat cubes in small amount of vegetable oil in iron skillet. Remove meat, then brown onions in same skillet. Add salt, pepper and garlic. Mix meat and onions in iron Dutch oven. Heat beef broth in skillet where meat and onions were browned. Scrape bottom for brown crusty pieces and pour over meat and onions. Add brown sugar, thyme, bay leaves and parsley. Add beer until meat is barely covered. Cook in Dutch oven at 325 degrees for 2 hours, 30 minutes. Dissolve cornstarch in wine vinegar and add to mixture to thicken gravy. Serve over rice.

Sipsey River Bottom Chili

Serves: 4
Prep Time: 4 hours

1 **lb. ground venison**
1 **large onion, chopped**
1 **green pepper,
chopped**
2 **T. vegetable oil**
2 **T. brown sugar
dash of paprika
dash of cayenne
pepper**
1 **large can tomato
sauce**
1 **cup water**
1½ **T. salt**
2 **T. chili powder**
1 **tsp. Worcestershire
sauce**
1 **T. catsup**
1 **can kidney beans**

Brown onion, green pepper and venison in vegetable oil. Add
remaining ingredients (except beans) and simmer for 15
minutes. Add beans and simmer for 3 hours.

Country-Fried Venison Steaks And Gravy

Serves: 4
Prep Time: 30 minutes

**4 venison ham steaks,
¹/₂ inch thick
butter or margarine
1 cup milk
flour
salt and pepper to taste**

Pound steaks thoroughly with sharp-edged meat mallet. Cut into serving-size pieces. Melt butter to fill ¹/₄ inch on bottom of deep skillet. Dip steaks into milk and dredge in flour. Lightly brown one side in hot butter. Season meat with salt and pepper. Turn and let second side brown lightly. Remove steaks from skillet. Make gravy by adding flour to remaining butter, forming a paste. Gradually add remaining milk and salt and pepper to taste. Stir constantly until gravy begins to thicken. Additional milk or water can be added if thinner gravy is desired. Turn heat to low setting and add meat to gravy. Cover and simmer for about 5 minutes. Serve with mashed potatoes.

Camper's Venison

Serves: 4
Prep Time: 2 hours, 15 minutes

**2 lbs. venison, cubed
salt and pepper to taste
flour
4 T. butter or margarine
2 cups hot water
1 4-oz. can mushrooms
1 medium onion, sliced**

**3 medium carrots,
sliced
1 8-oz. can lima or
butter beans**

Season meat with salt and pepper and dredge with flour. Brown meat in butter or margarine in heavy frying pan over hot fire. After meat is browned, add hot water and vegetables. Cover and simmer about 2 hours or until meat is tender. Thicken with flour if desired.

Cross Creek Hollow Tender Roast

Serves: 12
Prep Time: 6 hours

1 7-lb. venison roast
1 pkg. meat marinade
1/4 cup water
  salt and pepper to taste
1 cup apple juice

Place meat in roasting pan. Mix meat marinade with water to make paste and spread over roast. Season meat with salt and pepper. Add apple juice to roasting pan. Cover and cook at 250 degrees for 6 hours or until desired doneness. Add apple juice as needed to keep roast moist.

Batter-Dipped Meatballs

Serves: 6
Prep Time: 2 hours

1½ lbs. ground venison
 ¼ cup beer
 1 egg
 1 tsp. salt
 ½ cup dried bread crumbs
 ¼ tsp. pepper
 2 T. onion, grated

Batter:
 ⅔ cup beer
 2 eggs
 4 tsp. salad oil
1⅓ cups flour
 1 tsp. baking powder
1½ tsp. salt
 ¼ tsp. pepper

Mix all ingredients (not batter) thoroughly and shape into 1-inch meatballs. Brown lightly in oven or in skillet and set aside. Prepare batter: In medium bowl, beat together beer, eggs and oil with fork. Stir in flour, baking powder, salt and pepper until well blended. Coat meatballs, a few at a time, with batter (batter is quite thick), and deep-fry in hot oil until golden brown. Drain meatballs and keep warm in oven until all are done. Serve with mustard sauce.

Cross Creek Hollow Jerky

Serves: 8
Prep time: 2 days

2 lbs. venison	**¹/₄ tsp. garlic powder**
1 pkg. meat marinade	**¹/₄ tsp. onion powder**
1 cup cold water	**¹/₄ tsp. black pepper**
¹/₂ tsp. liquid smoke	

Cut venison (with grain) into strips 1¹/₂ inches wide, ¹/₂ inch thick and 6 inches long. Trim off all fat. Set aside. Combine remaining ingredients and mix thoroughly. Place meat in glass container and cover with mixture. Cover and leave overnight in refrigerator. Remove strips and drain. Stick a round toothpick through one end of each strip. Place layer of aluminum foil in bottom of oven to catch drippings. Suspend strips from top oven rack. Turn heat to 120 degrees or lowest setting. Leave oven door slightly open so moisture can escape. Dry strips for 8 hours or until meat turns dark and there is no moisture in center of strips.

Glossary Of Essential Southern Cooking Terms
(with a few nonessential ones thrown in for fun)

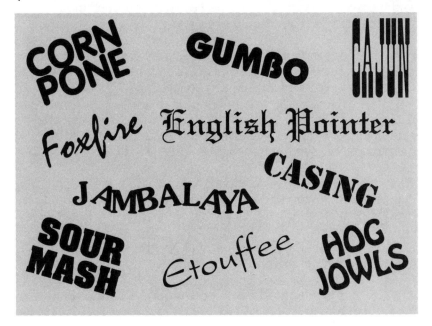

Should you find yourself in a Southern kitchen, general store or hunting camp, these terms should at least let you follow the conversation. Note carefully the terms for foods or situations you might want to avoid if you have tender sensibilities.

Andouille: Sausage used in cooking. Originally made using pieces of intestine or chitterlings stuffed into a large casing with pork (or ham), onions, garlic and cayenne, then smoked.

Bacon drippings: The fat that is rendered after bacon has been fried until crispy.

Bisque: A type of soup usually made with a cream base. In southern Louisiana, it is often made with a dark roux and crayfish, shrimp or fish, and highly seasoned.

Bloodying: The tradition in Southern deer camps of smearing a young hunter's face with the blood of his first deer.

Southern Cooking Glossary

Boucherie: French for "butchery." La boucherie evolved into a communal event where all participants shared the slaughtering and meat-preserving chores, then divided the fresh meat, lard and other smoked and salted products.

Cajun: A descendant of the original Acadian refugees or anyone absorbed into the Cajun culture by marriage or choice. Cajuns settled mostly in southern Louisiana.

Casing: The large or small intestines of an animal which are stuffed to make sausage. Casing can be purchased at most meat counters. Synthetic casings are also available.

Cayenne pepper: The very pungent fruit of a variety of capsicum. Fresh or pickled, ground or whole, this seasoning is used in cooking many foods.

Collard greens: The leaves of a stalked, smooth-leafed type of kale. Something like chard or spinach.

Corn bread: Bread made with cornmeal. It is also called Johnny cake.

Corn dodger: A cake of corn bread which is fried, baked or boiled as a dumpling.

Corn flour: Corn finely ground to the consistency of flour.

Cornmeal: Meal ground from corn. Several types are available, including regular yellow, white and self-rising. Be sure you have the right type for your recipe.

Corn pone: Corn bread often made without milk or eggs and baked or fried.

Creole: A term generally applied to a native-born descendant of Mediterranean ancestry.

Dash: A small amount of seasoning. Also what you do upon encountering a cottonmouth under your beached duck boat.

Egg-sucking son-of-a-____: Description of lineage of

following entry when quail are flushed out of range or dog refuses to retrieve from briar patch..

English pointer: The renowned quail dog of the South. Known for its beauty, dependability and incredible nose. Lauded in verse and song and valued by some Southern hunters more than spouse and offspring.

Etouffee: French for smothered. A dish made with onions, seasonings and meat, fish or vegetables smothered and slowly cooked.

Foxfire: The smell of gases generated by decay in the swamp. Noted only so that if your dinner guests arrive and say that the house smells like foxfire, you had better go out for pizza.

Fur Piece: A long way.

Green: The leaves of any root crop. Also, what you may turn upon discovering that your Southern host's family recipe for Brunswick stew includes the squirrels' heads, incisors and all.

Grillades: The lean strips of meat from the belly of a hog.

Gumbo: A soup made with a dark roux and water; also with seafood and meat. Eaten with rice.

Ham: Meat from the rear quarter of a hog. Often smoke cured. Also anyone who shoots three or more quail on a covey rise.

Hock: A small cut of meat from just above either the front or hind foot of a hog. Cured in brine to make the Southern delicacy, pickled pork hocks.

Hog jowls: The cheek meat from a hog. Prized in Southern cooking.

Holler: A valley or a gully. Often the sight of good hunting or good campfires. Also a good way to let off steam.

Hush puppy: Cornmeal dough shaped into small balls and deep fried in fat. Named because they were thrown to the dogs to keep them quiet during the family's meal.

Jambalaya: A dish from Louisiana consisting of rice, meat (or seafood), and other seasonings, cooked in one pot.

Julep: A traditional southern drink made with bourbon and sugar syrup, poured over crushed ice and garnished with mint.

Okra: A vegetable often boiled or stewed. Also used in gumbo.

Passle: That's with a "P" not an "H," though a passle of hungry hunters could sure make for a hassle.

Pope's nose: The fleshy protuberance at the posterior of a dressed fowl. Also called a parson's nose.

Roux: Flour browned in fat; used to thicken gravies, gumbos and sauces.

Salt pork: Fat pork cured in salt or bacon.

Sassafras: Medicinal tea and flavoring oils are made from its roots.

Shirttailin': The Southern deer camp tradition of forceably detaching and displaying prominently the shirttail of anyone dumb enough to miss a buck and tell his campmates about it!

Sour mash: Whiskey made from crushed corn stirred in hot water to ferment. Often used to ease the embarrassment by recipient of a shirttailin'.

Sow belly: Fat salt pork or bacon.

Spider: An alternate name for a black, cast-iron skillet. True spiders were made with short feet.

Turnip greens: The leaves from turnips. In the South, this part of the plant is considered more palatable than the roots.

Yawl: A person or group of people to whom you are speaking.

Upland Birds

The Mad Baron
Of Piney Wood Knoll

by John Phillips

The gobble of a wild turkey has a mystical, addictive power. The sound is as powerful as the wailing of the sirens whose seductive songs caused the ancients to sail their ships into disaster. The only remedy to counteract the lure of the sirens' melodies was discovered by the Greeks; they stuffed their ears with cotton. Likewise, ear stuffing may be the only way to keep a hunter from being lured to the madness caused by a wild turkey's gobble.

To say exactly why the gobble of a wild turkey has such addictive powers is difficult. Maybe it has something to do with the coming of spring. Like the mountain men of old who gathered for the rendezvous when winter's icy grip left the Rockies, perhaps turkey hunters are merely seeking a mascot who shares their joy for being alive. The wild turkey's gobble surely must be recognized everywhere as an expression of a zest for life and love!

Have you ever known a man who was in love with a beautiful woman to the point that she dominated his mind and his spirit? All the man could think about was that woman, but she didn't return his affection. That's exactly what happens to a turkey hunter when he hunts a wily gobbler that won't come to his calling. Like a love-sick teenager, many turkey hunters can't eat, sleep or think of anything but the gobbler they're chasing.

If you've played chess, you know that when you make a move, you not only have to determine how that move will work to your advantage but how that move can disadvantage your opponent. But, while deciding what to do next, you must also determine what to do if your opponent counters your move with one of several options. A good chess player makes his moves not only to win, but also to keep from losing.

The game of hunting turkey is much the same. For every move the hunter makes, the turkey can choose from an infinite number of countermoves. The advantage is much the gobbler's because the board on which he and the hunter are playing is the turkey's living room. He knows it far better than the hunter. Therefore, if the hunter only knows strategies that will help him win, but hasn't worked out tactics that will prevent him from losing, he will be defeated.

How consuming can turkey hunting become? Perhaps the tale of the Mad Baron of Piney Wood Knoll will reveal to non-turkey hunters the degree to which the spring gobbler *fever* affects dedicated turkey hunters.

There was once a gobbler, the Mad Baron of Piney Wood Knoll, that captured the minds of most of the male population of an entire Southern community. Every man and boy in the town thought that harvesting this legendary tom was his sacred calling.

Old timers recall that some of the town's most devoted husbands and wives were on the verge of divorce because this gobbler demanded more time from the men than the ladies received. Businesses, they say, were about to close because the Mad Baron kept the citizens of the community away from their work at least until noon each day of the turkey season.

And the young people? They couldn't even court each other proper because the young men spent every waking hour planning, plotting and conniving a scheme to take the Mad Baron.

Ambushes were laid, and assassination plots were planned, but season after season went by and the Mad Baron was never cornered.

One year, there was even one attempt to set fire to the woods and drive the Mad Baron out to the hunters. Snares were placed along game trails; trail timers were used to plot the course of the gobbler, but nothing ... nothing would catch the Mad Baron off guard.

The battle between this community—which shall remain nameless—and the Mad Baron was not simply a one-spring skirmish. The war raged for three years, resulting, some say, in seven divorces and 22 lost jobs. The tiny Southern town was shaken to its foundation. During the off-season, city fathers met late into the night struggling to hold the community together.

Realizing that there was little hope for the community unless the Mad Baron was removed, one wiry young man, sound of both body and mind, concocted the plan that would lead to the Baron's eventual demise. The plan was magnificent in its simplicity and its results.

"Well, I figured I either had to kill the Baron or stand by and watch my friends and hometown suffer," said Sage Thomas (name changed to protect the hero). "So I went to a friend in a nearby community who had a 10-gauge shotgun. You know, one of those special turkey models. Well, I borrowed that shotgun and three shells.

"Then I waited until the worst morning of the spring. At midnight the rain was pouring down, the sky was lit with lightning and the thunder rolled over town almost continuously.

In the wee hours of the morning, I went to the knoll where the Mad Baron began his gobbling every day. It was the spookiest place I ever seen or ever heard tell of! With the lightning flashing and the thunder crashing I didn't want to stay, but I clutched the Bible in my pocket and trudged on.

"Every time the thunder clashed, that turkey shock gobbled. Through the thick, smelly mud and incessant rain, I crawled on my belly like a snake to a small bush about 50 yards from where he was roosting. Under the cover of darkness and the storm, I hid in ambush and waited for the scourge of our town to fly down at first light.

"Every lightning flash silhouetted the Mad Baron in his giant water oak—a tree that had been his throne of terror for three long seasons. He was a terrible renegade responsible for ruinin' lives and leavin' little children orphaned, but I couldn't shoot him off that limb. Much as the town needed him finished, I couldn't have lived with the disgrace of taking the Mad Baron like that. So I waited beside that sparse bush in the pouring rain, and let me tell you daylight was mighty slow in comin' that particular day!

"When the white string of morning light was finally, slowly pulled across the black covers of darkness, that big tom ruffled his feathers, lifted his head, stretched his wings, let out a thunderous double gobble and pitched off the limb.

"As the Mad Baron's toenails touched the soft earth beneath his tree I squeezed the trigger of the 10 gauge, and the big cannon reported. At that range, there weren't no missin'.

"I returned to town and showed the Mad Baron to everyone, not to prove my prowess as a hunter, but rather to show the townsfolk that the villain was dead and that we could return to our everyday affairs of life.

"The only thing that worries me is that next spring one of the Mad Baron's many offspring will ascend to the oaken throne and continue where his daddy left off!"

Fried Doves

Serves: varies
Prep Time: 1 hour, 30 minutes

doves (number varies)	**1-2 cups white wine**
flour	**salt and pepper to taste**
butter	

Roll doves in flour. Melt butter in iron skillet and fry doves until brown. Add wine and simmer for 1 hour (or longer). Season with salt and pepper.

Robert Bender
Chambersburg, Pennsylvania

Dove And Rice Casserole

Serves: 4
Prep Time: 1 hour, 30 minutes

12 dove breasts, boned	**2 cups rice, uncooked**
1 lb. fresh mushrooms, thicky sliced	**1 onion, chopped**
12 small pearl onions	**2 T. chicken broth mix (powder or cube)**
12 bacon strips, thinly sliced	**salt and pepper to taste**
1/2 cup wild rice, partially cooked	**1 cup Marsala wine**
	water

Saute mushrooms. Make "sandwiches" with breast, mushrooms and pearl onions; hold together by wrapping with bacon. In 3-qt. casserole dish, mix wild rice, regular rice, chopped onion, chicken broth and salt and pepper. Arrange dove sandwiches (about 1/2 inch into rice), leaving spaces between them. Scatter remaining mushroom slices around doves. Pour wine over and add about 1 cup water. Bake at 400 degrees until rice is chewable and liquid is absorbed. Small amounts of additional liquid can be added if necessary.

William Heins
Red Bluff, California

Doves And Gravy On Rice

Serves: 4
Prep Time: 45 minutes

16 dove breasts	**3 lemons**
flour	**garlic salt**
butter	**seasoned pepper**
1 cup water	**salt and pepper to taste**

Place breasts (meat side up) in large skillet. Sprinkle flour on them and brown in butter. Add water and the juice from 3 lemons. Season to taste. Simmer (covered) for 20 minutes. (Do not overcook.) Remove doves to warming dish.

C.E. Kuempel
Pflugerville, Texas

Stir-Fry Grouse

Serves: 4
Prep Time: 30-40 minutes

2 grouse	**butter**
water	**1/2 cup frozen pea pods**
chicken bouillon	**1/2 cup frozen broccoli**
cornstarch (optional)	**1/2 cup green peppers,**
1/2 cup fresh mushrooms	**chopped**

Skin or pluck grouse and fillet meat from bone. Place meat in refrigerator. Put remaining bones and other scraps into small pot with about 1/2 cup water and chicken bouillon cube. Boil to a thick consistency. Saute mushrooms in butter. When mushrooms are about half done, in another frying pan, begin frying pea pods, broccoli and green peppers in oil on medium to high heat. Turn up heat on mushrooms to almost high. Cut up grouse breast into small pieces and add to mushrooms. Cook for about 1 minute on each side. When vegetables have cooked for 6-7 minutes and grouse is cooked, place meat, vegetables and gravy from stock pot into one pan and simmer for about 2 minutes.

Daniel Hobbs
Wisconsin Rapids, Wisconsin

Stuffed Grouse

Serves: 4
Prep Time: 2 hours

4 grouse
1 6-oz. pkg. long grain
and wild rice mix
½ cup celery, diced
1 5-oz. can water
chestnuts, sliced

1 3-oz. can chopped
mushrooms, drained
4 T. butter, melted
1 T. soy sauce

Cook rice. Cool. Add remaining ingredients (except grouse).
Toss ingredients lightly to mix. Salt inside of birds, stuff and
truss. Roast at 375 degrees (loosely covered) for 30 minutes.
Uncover and roast for 1 hour or until done.

Robert Shenk
Columbia, Pennsylvania

Grouse Casserole

Serves: 3
Prep Time: 1-2 hours

1-2 grouse
½ onion, chopped
vegetables, flaked
½ cup rice
1 pkg. broccoli

cream of celery soup
cream of chicken soup
American cheese slices
salt and pepper

Boil grouse in large pot of water with onion and vegetable
flakes for 1 hour. Remove grouse and discard water. Remove
bones from grouse and cut meat into pieces. Boil rice and cook
broccoli. Mix celery and chicken soups and add rice and
broccoli. Place grouse strips in casserole dish. Pour mixture
over grouse (to about 1 inch deep). Put cheese squares over
top. Place remaining grouse strips over cheese. Pour in
remaining mixture. Put cheese squares over top. Bake for about
15 minutes or until cheese melts. Season to taste.

John Smith
Fayetteville, Pennsylvania

Molokai Francolin (Hawaii)

Serves: 4
Prep Time: 30 minutes

6 Francolin's grouse	**¹/₂ cup macadamia nuts,**
2 cups Kiawe honey	**chopped**
1 cup barbecue sauce	

Mix barbecue sauce with honey to make glaze. Pluck, clean and dry grouse. Then, spread thick glaze over birds. (Put some on inside of cavity, too.) Place birds in greased casserole dish. Sprinkle macadamia nuts over birds and cover dish. Bake for 1 hour at 325 degrees.

Deane Gonzalez
Honolulu, Hawaii

Chuck's Taco Grouse

Serves: 2
Prep Time: 15-20 minutes

4-8 grouse breasts, boned	**2 tsp. Dijon mustard**
1 8-oz can tomato puree	**2 T. lime juice**
¹/₂ tsp. garlic, minced	**1¹/₂ T. light cooking oil**
¹/₂ tsp. ground coriander	**2 T. plain or nonfat**
1 tsp. ground cumin	**yogurt or sour cream**
¹/₂ tsp. medium or hot	
chili powder	

In medium bowl, mix tomato puree, garlic, coriander, cumin, chili powder and mustard. Wash and dry grouse breasts and dip in sauce. Heat oil in frying pan. Remove grouse from sauce and saute meat on medium-high heat until grouse turns light brown (1-2 minutes). Spoon part (or all) of leftover sauce over grouse and heat sauce. Place grouse on dinner plates and top with yogurt or sour cream. Serve with Spanish rice.

Charles Roberts
Mt. Vernon, Washington

Chuck's Grouse Breast With Sherry

Serves: 4
Prep Time: 15 minutes

4-8 grouse breasts   **4 T. butter or margarine**
   (depending on size)   **½ cup slivered almonds**
2 T. flour   **⅓ cup dry sherry**
½ tsp. salt   **¼ cup whipping cream**
¼ tsp. pepper

Wash and pat dry meat. Combine flour, salt and pepper. Dust meat with seasoned flour. Add 2 T. butter to skillet. Over medium heat, brown grouse (about 1-2 minutes per side). Remove grouse to warm platter. Add remaining butter or margarine and lightly brown slivered almonds. Turn almonds out onto platter with grouse meat. Add sherry to same pan. Bring to light boil and scrape pan. Add cream and simmer 2-3 minutes. Pour sherry cream over grouse and serve immediately.

Charles Roberts
Mt. Vernon, Washington

Grouse Breast With Wine And Rice

Serves: 2-3
Prep Time: 1 hour

1½ lbs. grouse, skinned,   **3 T. chives, chopped**
  boned and cut   **salt and pepper to taste**
¾ stick corn-oil margarine   **1 cup white wine**
2 garlic cloves, pressed   **1 cup rice**
1 cup onion, diced   **2 cups water**
1 cup celery, diced

Melt margarine in 3-qt. pot. Add garlic and saute 1-2 minutes. Add onion and celery and cook until translucent. Add meat and stir until white. Add chives, salt and pepper and wine. Cover and simmer for 45 minutes. Cook rice in 2 cups salted water for 20 minutes. To serve, spoon grouse breast mixture over rice.

Dick Greeno
Lowell, Massachusetts

Smoked Pheasant Sausage

Serves: 10
Prep Time: 8 hours

2 lbs. pheasant	**¹/₂ T. onion powder**
1¹/₄ lbs. pork cubes	**1 T. poultry seasoning**
1³/₄ bowl fat	**2 oz. white wine**
1 oz. salt	
¹/₄ T. curing salt	
¹/₄ T. white pepper	

Mix all ingredients together. Grind meat on medium grinder. Pipe into sheep casing. Make sausage 4¹/₂ inches long. Place on dry smoke for 7 hours.

Anthony Hebert
Patterson, New York

Baked Pheasant In Cream

Serves: 4
Prep Time: 1 hour

2 pheasant	**1 medium green pepper,**
salt to taste	**sliced in rings**
pepper to taste	**1 T. pimiento, sliced**
flour	**paprika**
cooking oil	
2 pts. half & half cream	

Clean pheasant and cut into serving-size pieces. Then, season with salt and pepper, and dust with flour. Cook in a well-oiled heavy skillet until brown. Remove meat, place in casserole and pour cream over top. If cream doesn't completely cover pieces, add canned milk (dilute with water). Place green pepper rings and pimiento on top of meat and bake at 350 degrees until meat is tender, about 1 hour. Sprinkle paprika on top and serve with mashed potatoes, green peas and fruit salad.

John Paulisin Sr.
Monroe, Connecticut

Pheasant Pecan

Serves: 6
Prep Time: 30 minutes

3-4 pheasant breasts	**1 cup pecans, finely**
2 egg yolks	**chopped**
3-4 T. water	**butter**
bread crumbs	

Pound breasts thin and roll them in flour. Combine egg yolks and water to form egg wash. On separate dish, combine pecans and a few bread crumbs. Then, dip meat in egg wash and roll in pecan mixture. Saute meat in butter until brown on both sides. Bake at 350 degrees for 10 minutes.

James King
Royal Oak, Michigan

Baked Pheasant With Cherry Sauce

Serves: 4
Prep Time: 40 minutes

2 pheasants, halved	**1 small jar currant jelly**
8 bacon strips	**2 T. cornstarch**
½ cup sugar	**1 T. water**
½ cup cherry liquor	**2 cans purple bing**
½ stick butter	**cherries, drained**
1 T. Worcestershire	
sauce	

Bake pheasants at 400 degrees for 20 minutes to brown quickly. Then, put 2 bacon strips on each half. For sauce: Combine sugar, cherry liquor, butter, Worcestershire sauce; add jelly. Cook until dissolved. Mix cornstarch and water; add to mixture. (This should be a little thicker than milk.) Add a little more water if necessary. Bring to a boil until thickened. Add cherries. Pour sauce over breasts and serve.

James King
Royal Oak, Michigan

Yam Hobo Pheasant

Serves: 2-4
Prep Time: 30-40 minutes

1 pheasant	**garlic to taste**
salt to taste	**aluminum foil**
pepper to taste	**1 12-oz. can candied yams**

Make a fire and let it burn to red coals. Season bird with salt, pepper and garlic. Put bird in aluminum foil and add can of yams. Wrap tightly and cook in fire (covered with coals) for about 40 minutes.

Jerry Wilson
Janesville, California

Uncle Rod's Hot Pheasant Stew

Serves: 4-6
Prep Time: 1 day

2-4 lbs. pheasant	**1 garlic clove, crushed**
salt	**1 handful mushrooms**
1 oz. olive oil	**1 red onion, chopped**
2 celery stalks, chopped	**2 medium jalapeno**
4 medium potatoes,	**peppers, chopped**
chunked (with skin on)	**oregano to taste**
3 carrots, chopped	**basil to taste**
1 can beans	**2 large cans V-8 juice**
1 can peas	**1 cup blush wine**

Boil pheasant in 6- to 8-qt. soup kettle. Salt the water and use shot of olive oil when meat starts to peel off bone. Take bird out of kettle and remove bones. Place meat back in kettle. Pour out juice, leaving enough to cover meat. In separate large kettle, combine all vegetables. Then, add salt and pepper, oregano and basil. Pour V-8 juice and wine over everything. Cover and simmer until potatoes and carrots are tender. Put meat and juice in at this time. Simmer 1 more hour. Serve with French bread.

Rod Williamson
Modesto, California

Pheasant And Mushrooms

Serves: 4-6
Prep Time: 2 hours

1 pheasant, cut up	**flour**
3 bacon slices, chopped	**½ cup mushroom liquid**
1 can sliced mushrooms	**and water**
1 small onion, chopped	**¼ cup sour cream**

Pan-fry bacon pieces until crisp, then remove to separate dish. Roll pheasant pieces in flour and brown in bacon grease. Arrange browned pheasant pieces in baking dish. Drain mushrooms, reserving liquid. Sprinkle bacon, onions and mushrooms over pheasant pieces. Season meat with salt and pepper. Combine mushroom liquid with water to make ½ cup. Add sour cream to mushroom liquid and mix thoroughly. Pour sour cream mixture over pheasant. Cover and bake at 350 degrees for 1 hour, 15 minutes or until tender.

DeLane Dollinger
Venturia, North Dakota

Pheasant Ala Hansen

Serves: 2
Prep Time: 1 hour, 30 minutes

1 pheasant	**2 onions, chopped**
salt and pepper	**1 tsp. sugar**
5 bacon slices	**1 pkg. mushrooms**
butter	**6 tsp. Madeira wine**

Rub pheasant with salt and pepper outside and inside. Place bacon on top of pheasant using toothpicks. Melt butter in large pot and cook pheasant for 5 minutes. Place pheasant in casserole dish and bake at 320 degrees for 15 minutes. Meanwhile, saute onion in butter and sugar for 5 minutes. Place mushrooms and onions around pheasant and cook (covered) for 50 minutes. Then, pour wine over pheasant.

Philip Dyhre Hansen
Cliffside Park, New Jersey

Pheasant Casserole

Serves: 4-6
Prep Time: 1 hour

24 oz. pheasant, cooked and cubed	**2 T. flour**
	1 cup mayonnaise
1 16-oz. can mushrooms	**1 tsp. seasoning salt**
1 small jar red pimiento	**1 can cream of**
½ cup onion, chopped	**mushroom soup**
1 cup celery, chopped	**8 hamburger buns**

Combine ingredients and place in casserole dish. Cover and bake at 375 degrees for 45 minutes. Serve over buns.

Carl Runke
Hutchinson, Minnesota

Pheasant Burgundy

Serves: 2-4
Prep Time: 1 hour, 15 minutes

1-2 pheasants, cut up	**1 onion, chopped**
1 cup flour	**2 garlic cloves, chopped**
salt and pepper to taste	**1 green pepper,**
3 T. olive oil	**chopped**
2 cups burgundy wine	**2 tomatoes, chopped**
2 cups water	**½ lb. mushrooms**
seasoning salt to taste	**10 olives, chopped**

Combine flour and salt and pepper. Coat pheasant with seasoned flour and brown on stove in large skillet with olive oil. When browned, add 1 cup wine and 1 cup water. Bring to a boil. Lower heat and simmer. When water and burgundy are half gone, add remaining cup of wine and water. Then, add seasoning salt, onion, garlic, green pepper, tomatoes, mushrooms and olives. Bring to slow boil. Lower heat, stir and cook until done. Add more wine and water if necessary. Serve over mashed potatoes with red wine, dinner rolls and butter.

Floyd Davis
Sacramento, California

Pheasant Silverado

Serves: 2-4
Prep Time: 2 hours

1-2 pheasants, cut up	1 cup sherry wine (dry
1/2 lb. fresh mushrooms,	preferred)
sliced or chopped	1/2 cup brandy
1 onion, chopped	1 tsp. seasoning salt
2 garlic cloves, chopped	pepper to taste
1 tomato, chopped	
(optional)	
1 16-oz. can chicken	
broth	

Preheat oven to 300 degrees. Combine all ingredients (except pheasant), mixing thoroughly. Add pheasant and place in large cooking pot. Bake at 300 degrees for 1 hour, 40 minutes or until meat falls off bone. Serve with brown wild rice, sliced cheese, tossed green salad, French bread and chilled white wine.

Floyd Davis
Sacramento, California

Roast Pheasant

Serves: 4-6
Prep Time: 3 hours

1 pheasant	1/2 tsp. salt
1/2 cup mushrooms,	1/4 tsp. celery salt
chopped	1/4 tsp. black pepper
1 tsp. onion, chopped	11/2 cups bread crumbs
1 T. butter	1/2 cup chicken broth
2 T. fresh parsley,	
chopped	

Clean pheasants. Mix ingredients together and stuff bird. Bake at 350 degrees for about 2-3 hours or until done.

Robert Bender
Chambersburg, Pennsylvania

Pheasant With Blue Cheese And Grapes

Serves: 4
Prep Time: 1 hour, 15 minutes

1 3-lb. pheasant	**1 lb. blue cheese,**
2 eggs, beaten	**crumbled**
2 cups bread crumbs	**2 pts. sour cream**
1 cup flour	**8 garlic cloves, crushed**
2 T. oil	**1/2 cup red or white**
2 T. butter	**grapes, seedless**

Cut pheasant into quarters. Mix eggs and bread crumbs together. Dredge pheasant in flour; then, roll in egg and bread crumb mixture. Brown pheasant in oil and butter. Put browned pheasant in baking dish and set aside. Mix blue cheese, sour cream and garlic. Pour mixture over pheasant, cover dish and bake at 350 degrees for 35-45 minutes. Remove pheasant and spoon on sauce.

James Distel
Philadelphia, Pennsylvania

Bourbon Smoked Pheasant

Serves: 2-4
Prep Time: 3 hours

1 2 1/2-3 lb. bird	**water**
4-6 hickory chunks or 4	**charcoal**
cups chips	**2 shots bourbon**

Soak chips for about 1 hour in water. Fill smoker 3/4 full with charcoal. Light fire. Let coals burn until white ashes are left. Place water bath above coals. Add hot water to pan. Add bourbon. On rack over water, add bird topside. Insert thermometer in bird's thigh. Don't touch bone. After draining wood, place on coals. Cover and cook about 1 hour, 30 minutes or until temperature in thigh is 180 degrees. (Add coals and wood as you go). Serve warm or chill. Great with garlic grilled potatoes or hot potato salad.

Walter Squier
Portland, Connecticut

Macaroni Pheasant Casserole

Serves: 2-4
Prep Time: 1 hour

1 **3-4 lb. pheasant**	1 **can cream of**
1 **8-oz. pkg. macaroni,**	**mushroom soup**
cooked	1/2 **tsp. salt**
1/2 **cup onions, chopped**	1/4 **tsp. pepper**
1/2 **cup green bell**	3/4 **lb. cheddar cheese,**
peppers, chopped	**grated**

Cut pheasant into small pieces. Place all ingredients (except cheese) in casserole dish, mixing thoroughly. Sprinkle grated cheese on top. Cover and bake at 350 degrees for 45 minutes.

Joe Depaolantonio
Colorado Springs, Colorado

Pheasants With Cream

Serves: 6-8
Prep. Time: 2 hours, 30 minutes

4 **pheasants, halved or**	**salt and fresh ground**
quartered	**pepper to taste**
butter	**mushrooms**
1/3 **bottle brandy**	3 **cups heavy cream**
2 **cups chicken broth**	1 **5-oz. jar horseradish**
1 **small onion, chopped**	1/2 **tsp. poultry seasoning**
1 **garlic clove, pressed**	

Brown pheasants in butter in oven-proof frying pan. Add brandy to birds and ignite—be careful. Let flames die. Add broth, onion, garlic and salt and pepper. Bake at 300-325 degrees for 30 minutes. Baste several times while baking. Add cream and horseradish to taste. Bake 1 hour, 30 minutes turning often. Saute mushrooms in butter and add to pan liquid. Serve mushrooms over pheasants.

Walter Squier
Portland, Connecticut

Crocked Pheasant

Serves: 4
Prep Time: 3-5 hours

4-6 pheasant breasts	**³/₄ cup celery, diced**
1 can cream of mushroom soup	**¹/₂ cup green pepper, diced**
1 can cream of chicken soup	**dash of Worcestershire sauce**
1 can cream of celery or cheddar cheese soup	**1¹/₄ cups instant rice**
	¹/₂ can water or white wine

Combine all ingredients (except breasts). Pour mixture into a well-buttered Crockpot or slow cooker. Add breasts on top. Cook 3-4 hours on high or 4-5 hours on low. Add liquid if it gets a little dry.

Walter Squier
Portland, Connecticut

Pheasant, Chili And Rice Casserole

Serves: 4
Prep Time: 1 hour

2 cups pheasant	**¹/₂ lb. Monterey Jack cheese, grated**
2 cups rice, cooked	
1 small can whole green chilis, seedless	

Sauce:

1 10 ³/₄-oz. can cream of chicken soup	**1¹/₂ tsp. garlic salt**
1 cup sour cream	**1 tsp. paprika**
	1 tsp. oregano

In 9x13-inch pan, layer rice, pheasant, chilis, sauce and grated cheese. Heat thoroughly at 350 degrees.

James Hendricks
Lakeside, California

Quick Italian Pheasant

Serves: 4
Prep Time: 1 hour

 2 **pheasants, dressed
   and quartered**
 ½ **stick margarine,
   melted**
 2 **pkgs. dry Italian salad
   dressing mix**
 1 **cup Italian seasoned
   bread crumbs**

Dip pheasant parts in melted margarine. Combine bread
crumbs and dressing mix and dip pheasant in this mixture.
Coat well. Place in buttered glass baking dish. Bake for about
35 minutes at 375 degrees.

Bill Miller
Chaska, Minnesota

Joyce's Sauteed Ptarmigan

Serves: 2
Prep Time: 30 minutes

 3 **ptarmigan breasts**   ¼ **tsp. garlic powder**
   salt and pepper to taste   1 **cup dry white wine**
   cornstarch   ½ **cup water**
 1 **large onion, sliced**
 1 **T. butter or margarine**

Fillet ptarmigan breasts and slice with the grain into thin strips.
Season strips with salt and pepper and dredge in cornstarch. In
frying pan, saute onion in melted butter until half done. Add
ptarmigan and cook until brown. Sprinkle garlic powder over
meat, then add wine and water. Cover and simmer until done.

Bill Iliff
FPO Seattle, Washington

Quail Stew

Serves: 6-8
Prep Time: 2 hours

> **1 quail, cut into small**
> **pieces**
> **cooking oil**
> **1 T. pepper**
> **1 T. salt**
> **2 T. garlic powder**
> **4 potatoes, chopped**
> **2 celery stalks, chopped**
> **2 carrots, chopped**
> **1 onion, diced**

In skillet over low heat, brown quail in oil. In separate 8-qt. pan, combine remaining ingredients. Add quail to pan and simmer on medium heat for 2 hours or until potatoes are tender.

Dwayne Warner Sr.
Yucca Valley, California

French-Fried Quail

Serves: 6
Prep Time: 15 minutes

> **6 quail**
> **2 4-oz. pkgs. saltine**
> **crackers, crumbled**
> **Schilling's Salad**
> **Supreme seasoning**
> **salt and pepper to taste**
> **2 eggs, beaten**

Fillet quail breasts. Combine crackers, seasoning and salt and pepper. Cover quail fillets with eggs, then roll in seasoned saltine crumbs and drop into hot (375 degrees) deep-fat fryer. Cook in fat for about 1 minute, 30 seconds.

Carl Runke
Hutchinson, Minnesota

Quail Veronique

Serves: 6
Prep Time: 1 hour

6 quail, cleaned	**juice from 1 lemon**
seasoned flour	**1/2 cup seedless grapes**
1/2 cup sweet butter	**1/2 cup pine nuts**
1 cup dry white wine	**hot wild rice**

Rub quail with seasoned flour. Saute birds in butter until golden brown. Add wine and lemon juice. Cover and cook over low heat for 15-20 minutes. Add grapes and pine nuts. Cook for another 10 minutes or until birds are tender. Spoon sauce over birds. Serve with hot wild rice.

Benjamin Weidling Sr.
Mauston, Wisconsin

Bobwhite Garden Delight

Serves: 6
Prep Time: 1 hour

12 bobwhite quail	**1 onion, chopped**
5 T. butter	**2 celery stalks,**
2 T. vegetable oil	**chopped**
1/4 cup dry white wine	**1/2 lemon, juiced**
2 carrots, thinly sliced	**parsley, chopped**
1/2 lb. fresh mushrooms	

Season quartered quail with salt and pepper. Heat 2 T. butter and oil in large skillet over medium heat. Add birds and cook 2 minutes on each side until golden brown. Drain on paper towels. Return skillet to heat and boil wine for 1-2 minutes. Stir constantly. Return birds and cook (covered) for 10 minutes at 450 degrees. Melt remaining butter in large saucepan. Add vegetables and lemon juice. Cook vegetables over medium heat for 5-10 minutes, stirring frequently. Add vegetables to skillet and cook until quail are tender. Garnish with parsley.

Dave VanOrden
Glencoe, Minnesota

Snipe On Toast

Serves: 8
Prep Time: 15-20 minutes

8 snipe, skinned	**1 T. butter**
flour	**1 T. flour**
3 T. peanut oil	**¹/₂ tsp. thyme**
¹/₄ cup fresh parsley	**1 cup sherry wine**
1 medium onion	**¹/₂ tsp. salt**
1 cup mushrooms	**¹/₂ tsp. pepper**

Dredge snipe in flour, then brown in peanut oil; set aside. Saute parsley, onions and mushrooms in butter until onions are translucent. Add 1 T. flour and saute for 2 minutes. Combine remaining ingredients, and add to sauteed ingredients. Cook until mixture thickens, stirring constantly. Place snipe on toast and ladle with sauce. Serve.

Robert Shenk
Columbia, Pennsylvania

BBQ Turkey Loaf

Serves: 6
Prep Time: 1 hour, 30 minutes

2¹/₂ lbs. wild turkey meat,	**1 onion, finely chopped**
ground	**1 egg**
1 cup cracker crumbs	**¹/₃ cup catsup**
1 cup barbecue potato	**¹/₄ cup barbecue sauce**
chip crumbs	**1 T. mustard**
1 cup mozzarella	**2 cups water**
cheese, shredded	

Combine cracker crumbs, potato chip crumbs and cheese in large mixing bowl. Add onion and turkey meat. Then, add egg, barbecue sauce, catsup and mustard. Season with salt and pepper. Mix thoroughly. Shape into loaf and place in glass baking dish. Add water and bake at 350 degrees for 1 hour.

Kirby Brought
Middleburg, Pennsylvania

Turkey Cabbage Rolls

Serves: 8
Prep Time: 1 hour

1 lb. turkey meat,
  freshly ground
8 large cabbage leaves
2 T. vegetable oil
1 cup fresh cabbage,
  chopped
1/2 cup onion, minced
1/2 cup carrot, minced
1/4 cup celery, minced
1 tsp. salt
1 tsp. dill weed
2 eggs
1/2 tsp. Tabasco sauce
1/2 cup fresh bread
  crumbs
1/3 cup butter

1/3 cup flour
2 cups chicken broth
2 T. lemon juice
2 tsp. lemon rind,
  grated
1/4 cup parsley, chopped

Cook cabbage leaves for 6 minutes in boiling water. Drain, pat dry and set aside. Heat oil in small skillet; add chopped cabbage, onion, carrot, celery, salt and 1/2 tsp. dill. Cook until vegetables tenderize. Beat eggs and Tabasco sauce together in medium bowl; mix in turkey, bread crumbs and cooked vegetable mixture. Divide turkey mixture into 8 sections; place one section in center of each cabbage leaf. Fold side of cabbage leaf toward center over filling; then, fold and overlap ends to make a small bundle. Fasten with toothpicks. Put cabbage rolls in 10x8x1¾-inch baking dish. To prepare sauce, melt butter in small saucepan, blend in flour and gradually add chicken broth. Cook over low heat, stirring constantly until thickened. Add lemon juice, lemon rind and remaining dill. Pour sauce over cabbage rolls. Cover and bake at 375 degrees for 40 minutes. Remove toothpicks before serving. Garnish with parsley.

Benjamin Weidling Sr.
Mauston, Wisconsin

Gas-Grilled Wild Turkey

Serves: varies
Prep Time: 3-5 hours

1 **wild turkey, plucked
   and cleaned
   butter, softened
   garlic powder to taste
   seasoning salt to taste
   pepper to taste**

Work butter between breast meat and breast skin. (Do this by pulling the skin up gently at the neck opening and the "back" opening. Be careful not to break the skin if possible. Work your hand all the way through with the butter, putting a layer of butter between breast meat and skin in all places you can reach.) Then, take more butter and cover outside of skin entirely. Season with spices (use more than normal). If you happen to tear the skin, use a toothpick to pin it to the breast. Then, take a piece of tinfoil and double it up so it is a little bigger than the breast portion. Cover breast with foil, tucking the edges around the front. Put turkey in pan, breast-side up, and fill bottom with water. Put thermometer in breast; do not touch any bone.

Place turkey on one side of preheated gas grill (medium-low temperature) away from direct heat. Let turkey cook until thermometer reaches 130 degrees. Then, remove tinfoil and let breast brown at about 170 degrees. (The breast should be a golden brown.) Let turkey cool for 10 minutes and carve. (A 16 lb. turkey takes about 4-5 hours.)

Daniel Hobbs
Wisconsin Rapids, Wisconsin

Other Big Game

Bear Hunt Diary

by Jim Shockey

Did you ever have one of those days? How 'bout one of those lifetimes? I'll guess the answer is "yes," because "Murphy's Law" is no stranger to hunters.

To help you feel better, here's the tale of one of my recent bear hunts through the eyes of two different beholders.

Husband's Diary
Entry Number 915
Night Before The Hunt:

Everything ready and laid out on kitchen table for easy, efficient access in morning. Tub of rotten meat and bone scraps in trunk of car. Must remember to fill bait barrel upon arriving at stand.

Prepare for early bedtime, although anti-hunting wife wishes to discuss honorable sport of bowhunting for vicious black bear. Must look up Webster's definition of discuss ... Neighbors three blocks away phone with request for wife to "discuss" in lower tone.

Man or mouse? Finally decide enough is enough ... declare self winner of discussion ... wife declares self winner of fight. Winner ... Ha! Know exactly how to get even. Wipe bleeding nose on wife's favorite white bathrobe in closet. Satisfied ... sleep soon after.

Wife's Diary:
Entry Number 915
Night Before The Hunt:

Husband finally moves stinky, rotten tub of dead stuff from garage. Decide to help husband renounce inhumane blood cause ... decide sick man simply enjoys violence. Clearly win discussion ... and fight ... nice left hook. Husband goes to bed early ... watch closely for signs of concussion.

Sleeping face much too smug. Decide to get even with face ... hide face's bow and arrows.

Husband's Diary
Entry Number 916
Morning Of Hunt:

Up three hours before dawn. Thankful everything prepared night before. Too groggy to think ... possible discussion concussion? Suddenly afraid about wife's bathrobe. Decide to take along. Will drop off at drycleaners on way home.

Begin loading gear into car. First take garbage bag filled with camp clothes and four relatively fresh, scent masking cow pies. Will not put camo on until arrival at tree stand. For trip in car and walk to stand, wear rubber galoshes on feet and full length rubber raincoat over underwear. Can never be too careful about leaving scent trail to tree stand.

Before leaving house, take care of one last secret detail.
Average human loses 40 hairs off head per day ... slightly
higher on own head. Own secret solution: Pull pair of wife's
panty hose over head. Too loose. Pull and pull until head
reaches ankle of hose ... finally fits head. Check clock. If hurry,
just enough time to be on stand by daybreak.

Drive fast, reach outskirts of town before realizing cannot
remember loading bow and arrows in car. Must pull U-turn and
speed home. Too much speed for own good. Almost home
when stopped by alert policeman. Driver's license in wallet, in
pocket of camo clothes. Try to reach into garbage bag. Officer
suddenly excited ... even through panty hose, pointy end of
officer's gun cold on nose. Offer to let excited policeman get
wallet by self. Officer obviously not bowhunter, reaches in bag
of camo clothing without looking first. Decide handful of
relatively fresh cow doo-doo good for masking scent ... bad for
chances of talking way out of speeding ticket.

Red, shaking officer wipes smelly hand on uniform ... angry,
definitely not a bowhunter. Requests explanation. Point back
over shoulder and say self headed out of town for day of bear
hunting with bow and arrow. Officer requests to see bow and
arrow. Ha, Ha. Officer would you believe self forgot bow? Self
in a lot of trouble.

Officer very understanding, removes gun from nose, steps
back. Holds gun in both hands. Self now knows how target
feels. Officer nice to let self out of car to stretch legs. Funny ...
wants self to turn back and stretch arms as well. Surprised to
feel officer's cold hands patting inside of legs ... officer
surprised to find no pants under rain coat.

Oh-Oh! Officer requests self lay face down on ground, arms
above head, legs spread. Self extremely concerned about
officer's intentions. Whew! No worry. Officer looking in back
seat of car. Finds packsack. Looks inside carefully this time
before reaching in. Pulls out plastic bag filled with white
powder ... Cocaine??? Self explain baking soda necessary to
rub all over body to avoid detection. Officer more interested in
wife's blood stained bathrobe. Moves to back of car and opens
trunk. Sees axe, shovel and tub of rotten meat.

Officer talks into walkie talkie. Overhear self referred to as "sick" many times. Appreciate officer's concern for health. Not sick yet. However, will be soon if continue to lay on cold ground wearing only underwear and rubber coat.

Soon many policemen ... and many guns. Given first ride in police car. At station, informed I have killed and chopped up wife. Cannot remember killing wife. But, know darn well all of wife would never fit in tub ... bathtub, maybe. Anyway, no need for concern, one call to wife will straighten matter out. First day of bear hunt gone. No problem, still three weeks left in season.

Wife's Diary
Entry Number 916
Morning Of Hunt:

Wake when husband does ... pretend to be asleep. Not completely satisfied with conclusion of previous night's discussion. Concussion did not knock more sense into husband as hoped.

Have new plan to get more even. When husband gone, pack bag and call taxi for lift to airport. Three weeks in resort on coast. Time for husband to forget bear and remember wife. Leave no forwarding note.

Peppered Antelope Roast

Serves: 2-4
Prep Time: 2 hours, 30 minutes

**1 4-lb. boneless
antelope roast, rolled
2 medium garlic cloves
vegetable oil
cracked black pepper
bacon slices**

Heat oven to 325 degrees. Cut each garlic clove into 4 or 5 slivers. Make 8 or 10 shallow slits in roast. Insert a garlic sliver into each slit. Place roast on rack in roasting pan and brush with oil. Sprinkle pepper liberally over roast. Cover roast with bacon slices. Roast to desired doneness, 22-32 minutes per pound. Allow meat to cool 10-15 minutes before carving. Serve with pan juices.

Denise Reynoldson
Kimball, Nebraska

Antelope Meatloaf

Serves: 4-6
Prep Time: 1 hour, 20 minutes

**2 lbs. ground antelope
(or any wild meat)
1 envelope dry onion
soup mix
1 egg
1/2 onion, finely chopped**

**1 tsp. Worcestershire
sauce
2 4-oz. cans tomato
sauce
1/4 cup brown sugar**

In mixing bowl, blend ground meat, soup mix, egg, onion and Worcestershire sauce. Form into loaf and place in 13x9-inch baking pan. Combine tomato sauce and brown sugar, then pour over meatloaf. Bake at 350 degrees for 1 hour.

Lt. Wilhelm Spicker
FPO New York

Paul's Antelope Meatloaf

Serves: 4
Prep Time: 1 hour

1 lb. antelope burger, ground	**¹⁄₄ cup green pepper, diced**
1 cup flavored (Italian) bread crumbs	**1 tsp. salt**
2 eggs, beaten	**¹⁄₄ tsp. pepper**
¹⁄₂ cup onion, minced	**2 cups tomato sauce**
	cooking oil

Combine antelope meat, bread crumbs, eggs, onion, green pepper, salt, pepper and 1 cup tomato sauce. Knead mixture until combined. Put light coat of cooking oil in loaf pan. Shape mixture into loaf, put in pan and bake at 350 degrees for 30 minutes. Then, pour remaining tomato sauce over loaf and bake another 30 minutes. Slice and serve with pasta.

Paul Blanda
Charlestown, Rhode Island

Bear Tips Ala Bob

Serves: 4-6
Prep Time: 1 hour, 30 minutes

3-5 lbs. bear sirloin tips	**2 lbs. fresh mushrooms, sliced**
1 jar Italian Salad dressing (not creamy)	**1 large garlic clove, chopped**
2 green peppers, chopped	**¹⁄₄ lb. butter**
1 medium onion, diced	**1 red pepper, crushed**

Marinate meat for at least 24 hours in Italian dressing. Cook meat over medium heat in frying pan. In separate bowl, combine peppers, onion and mushrooms. Melt butter and saute garlic. Add above vegetables with red pepper to taste. Remember to cook meat in marinade. Serve with baked potato and French bread.

Robert Pasquale
Wilmington, Massachusetts

Savory Bear Meatballs

Serves: 6 dinners or 18 hors d'oeuvres
Prep Time: 1 hour, 30 minutes

2 **lbs. ground bear**	½ **cup instant rice**
1 **egg**	2 **T. cooking oil**
1 **pkg. onion soup**	1 **10½-oz. can cream of**
1 **dash salt**	**mushroom soup**
1 **tsp. black pepper**	½ **cup sour cream**
1 **T. dried parsley**	

In mixing bowl, combine first seven ingredients. Shape into golf-ball-sized meatballs. In Dutch oven, brown meatballs in cooking oil. Remove from pan. Add soup and sour cream to meat drippings. Thin with water to desired consistency. When liquid is mixed, add meatballs. Reduce heat to low temperature and cover pan. Cook for 1 hour or until meatballs are done.

Lt. Wilhelm Spicker
FPO New York

Roast Bear Paws

Serves: 4
Prep Time: 4 hours

4 **small bear paws,**	1 **tsp. allspice**
skinned	**salt and pepper**
seasoned flour	2 **onions, thinly sliced**
3 **T. bacon fat**	4 **salt pork slices**
1 **tsp. cinnamon**	1 **cup water**

Roll paws in seasoned flour. Melt bacon fat in skillet, and brown paws. Put browned paws in casserole dish and sprinkle cinnamon, allspice and salt and pepper over them. In same bacon fat, cook onions until transparent. Arrange onions around paws in casserole dish, and lay salt pork slices on top. Pour water around paws. Place casserole dish in oven (covered) and roast at 350 degrees for about 4 hours.

Mark Slack
Eureka, California

Colorado River Bear Roast

Serves: 3-4
Prep time: 4 hours

1 **5-lb. bear roast**	1 **red onion, chopped**
salt and pepper	1 **celery bunch, chopped**
3 **garlic cloves**	1/2 **cup red wine**
2 **carrots, sliced**	

Rub salt and pepper on all sides of roast. Put roast in roaster or large Dutch oven, making several 1/2-inch cuts on top of roast. Put garlic into cuts. Add mixed vegetables on top of roast. Slowly pour wine over roast and vegetables. Marinate for 2 hours. Bake in preheated oven at 450 degrees for 40 minutes. Reduce heat to 300 degrees and cook for 1-2 hours until tender. Serve with mashed potatoes and brown gravy.

Dion Luke
Glenwood Springs, Colorado

Moist Boar Roast

Serves: 8-12
Prep Time: 24 hours plus 2 hours, 30 minutes

5-8 **lbs. boar roast**	3/4 **cup soy sauce or**
4-5 **garlic cloves, minced**	**teriyaki sauce**
1/2 **tsp. cinnamon**	1 **small can pineapple**
1/2 **tsp. cloves**	1 **oven roasting bag**
2 **tsp. dry mustard**	

Combine garlic cloves, cinnamon, cloves, dry mustard and soy sauce with pineapple juice for marinade. (Save pineapple rings.) Marinate roast for at least 24 hours, turning and basting frequently. Place roast (with pineapple rings on top) in oven roasting bag. Bake at 350 degrees for 1-2 hours. Let stand in bag for 10 minutes prior to slicing.

Diane Schmidt
Clovis, California

Gourmet Boar Chops

Serves: 6
Prep. Time: 1 hour, 30 minutes

6 boar chops	**½ tsp. ground ginger**
2 T. flour	**¼ tsp. dried rosemary,**
1 tsp. salt	**crushed**
⅛ tsp. pepper	**1 can French-fried**
2 T. shortening	**onions**
1 small can condensed	**½ cup sour cream**
mushroom soup	

Coat chops with mixture of flour, salt and pepper. In skillet, brown meat on both sides in hot shortening. Place meat in baking dish. In separate bowl, combine soup, ¾ cup water, ginger and rosemary. Pour mixture over chops. Sprinkle half the onions over meat. Cover and bake at 350 degrees for 50 minutes. Uncover and sprinkle remaining onions over chops. Continue baking for 10 minutes. Remove chops to platter. Blend sour cream into soup mixture. Heat mixture and serve with chops.

Robert Shenk
Columbia, Pennsylvania

Wild Boar From Denmark

Serves: 4
Prep Time: 30 minutes

4 boar chops	**salt**
4 tomatoes	**pepper**
butter	**bacon slices**

Cut a cross on top of tomatoes. Place some butter in each tomato. Melt some butter in skillet. Place tomatoes in skillet and cook (covered) for 5 minutes. Season chops with salt and pepper. Melt more butter in another skillet and cook chops for 4 minutes on each side. Fry bacon and place on top of chops with tomatoes on the side. Serve with potatoes.

Philip Hansen
Cliffside Park, New Jersey

Wild Boaritos

Serves: 4
Prep Time: 30 minutes

2 cups left-over boar roast, shredded	1 large can diced chilis
	1 medium bottle salsa
3-4 garlic cloves, minced	1 cup red onion, chopped
olive oil	1 cup cheese, grated
1 large can refried beans	12 tortillas

Saute garlic in olive oil. Add boar meat and stir until heated.
Add remaining ingredients (except tortillas) and simmer until
heated. Spread mixture on warm tortillas and roll into "boarito."
Enjoy.

Diane Schmidt
Clovis, California

Hawaiian Wild Boar—German Style

Serves: 20-30
Prep Time: 1 hour, 30 minutes

1 15-20-lb. wild boar hind quarter, boneless	1/4 tsp. nutmeg
salt and pepper	12 cloves
8 apples, grated	1/2 tsp. ground cinnamon
1 gal. red sauerkraut	

Season roast with salt and pepper in Dutch oven to lock in
moisture. Then, place roast in roasting pan. Combine apples
and red sauerkraut, mixing in nutmeg, cloves and cinnamon.
Place roast in baking pan and pour red sauerkraut mixture over
it. Cover pan and bake for 8 hours at 150 degrees. Then, raise
oven temperature to 200-225 degrees and bake an additional 2
hours. Serve with poi or mashed potatoes.

Deane Gonzalez
Honolulu, Hawaii

Squealing Good Pork

Serves: several
Prep Time: 10-12 hours

1 **150-200-lb. whole pig**	6 **burlap bags, soaked in**
1 **10-lb. bag salt**	**hot water**
lava rocks or oven	1 **3x8-ft. chicken**
bricks (with holes)	**wire**
6 **boxes lettuce leaves**	1 **gal. barbecue sauce**

Clean, shave and salt pig thoroughly. Make a pit approximately 1½ feet deep, and 5 feet wide. Put wood and rocks on top. Light wood and rocks, and let burn until rocks are red. Line rocks with leaves, covering well. Put some rocks in pig's belly. Tie pig to wire and carry. Place pig on top of leaves. Then, cover pig with rest of leaves and burlap and dirt, making a 1-2-foot mound. Cook for 11-12 hours. Serve with barbecue sauce.

Daniel Delisle
Haddon Field, New Jersey

BBQ Javelina Special

Serves: several
Prep Time: overnight plus 6 hours

1 **large javelina ham**	5 **lbs. charcoal**
1 **can beer**	**aluminum foil**
1 **8-oz. bottle Italian**	1 **large red onion, sliced**
dressing	**barbecue sauce**

Soak meat in mixture of beer and dressing overnight in refrigerator, turning once or twice. Prepare charcoal in 55-gal. drum pit. When all coals are gray (about 1 hour), place meat on grill, basting with beer and dressing mixture. Turn and baste every 10-15 minutes. After 1 hour, remove meat from grill. Place meat in double thickness foil. Pour about half of remaining baste over meat. Place onion slices on top and grill for 4 hours.

John Lopez
Galveston, Texas

Bill's Boar Ain't A Bore

Serves: 4
Prep Time: 2 hours

2-3 lbs. wild pork steak, thin
¼ cup clover honey
¼ cup sorghum or molasses
2 T. soy sauce
2 T. lemon juice
2 T. melted butter
cinnamon
ground cloves
garlic salt
white pepper
cayenne pepper (optional)
heavy cotton twine

Lay out steak flat in large baking dish with 4 ample lengths of twine laced in a tic-tac-toe pattern underneath meat. Mix honey, sorghum, soy sauce, lemon juice and melted butter. Because honey and sorghum are likely to be thick, heating the ingredients in a double boiler first eases blending. Drizzle this mixture heavily over steak until entire surface is covered. Shake on dry ingredients to taste. If cayenne pepper is used, shake on sparingly to avoid covering flavors of other ingredients.

Roll steak lengthwise, but try to keep ends tucked in (to avoid ingredients from running out). This is a messy procedure and is most easily accomplished with two sets of hands. Try to keep liquid from running out as much as possible, yet roll tightly. Tie steak into roll or ball with string. Be sure to tie securely. Place meat roll on barbecue rotisserie skewer and secure in place with prongs. Place over medium heat barbecue grill and turn on rotisserie for approximately 1 hour to 1 hour, 20 minutes. As with all pork or bear, be sure it is cooked thoroughly to avoid trichinosis. A meat thermometer is helpful in telling internal temperature.

Remove meat from skewer, slice thin and serve hot with biscuits and your favorite vegetable.

Bill Miller
Chaska, Minnesota

Elk Cheese Balls Grande

Serves: 5-10
Prep Time: 30 minutes

¹/₂ lb. ground elk
¹/₂ lb. ground round
1 lb. cheddar cheese

1 cup dry pancake mix
hot sauce or cayenne
pepper (optional)

Prepare ground elk meat and round for sausage. Add cheddar cheese and dry pancake mix. Mix thoroughly. Roll into small (tablespoon size) balls. Put rolls on cookie sheet. Bake for 15 minutes at 375 degrees. (Make sure some fat is added or in ground round.) Add a little hot sauce or cayenne pepper.

Bill Shipton
Las Cruces, New Mexico

Fireside Bliss

Serves: 4-6
Prep Time: 2 hours, 30 minutes

2 lbs. elk, 1-inch thick
1 pkg. beef-onion
  soup mix
1 1¹/₂-lb. can tomatoes
¹/₄ tsp. salt

1 T. cornstarch
¹/₂ cup juice from
  tomatoes
6 small onions
4 carrots, chunked

Tear off 20-inch sheet of heavy-duty aluminum foil and place in shallow pan. Cut elk into serving portions. Place elk on foil, overlapping slightly. Sprinkle soup mix and spoon tomatoes over meat. Mix seasonings with cornstarch and add to tomato juice. Pour juice mixture over meat and tomatoes. Arrange onions and carrots around meat. Bring two long ends of foil up over meat and seal with double fold. Seal remaining ends the same way, making a tight package. Place on middle shelf in oven. Bake at 350 degrees for 2 hours (or 5 hours at 250 degrees). Transfer package to serving dish and turn back foil.

Ralph Giaccio
Renton, Washington

Steak Salad

Serves: 6
Prep Time: 1 hour, 20 minutes

2 lbs. elk, boneless	**¹/₂ tsp. oregano**
¹/₄ cup vinegar	**¹/₂ tsp. black pepper**
¹/₄ cup red wine	**¹/₂ tsp. rosemary leaves**
¹/₄ cup olive oil	**1 onion, chopped**
1 garlic clove, minced	**12 cherry tomatoes**
1 jar artichoke hearts	**1 cup fresh mushrooms**
1 tsp. sugar	**5 cups fresh spinach**

Whisk vinegar and wine into olive oil, adding garlic, liquid from artichoke hearts, sugar, salt, pepper and herbs. Add steak, onion, tomato and sliced mushrooms. Marinate for 1 hour. Arrange spinach in bowl. Add marinated ingredients and artichoke hearts and toss. Spoon marinade over salad and serve.

Lawrence Meyer
Clancy, Montana

Stir-Fry Elk And Broccoli

Serves: 4
Prep Time: 30 minutes

1 lb. elk sirloin, cut up	**¹/₂ cup chicken broth**
vegetable oil	**2 T. soy sauce**
¹/₂ cup onion, diced	**2 tsp. cornstarch**
1 lb. fresh broccoli	**4 fresh tomatoes**

In wok or skillet, brown elk pieces in hot oil. When browned, remove and drain elk. Cook onion in oil until tender. Add onion to elk and set aside. Stir-fry broccoli until partially tender. Combine broth, soy sauce and cornstarch in small bowl. Add reserved elk and onions to broccoli in pan, pour broth mixture over all. Stir to mix. Simmer (covered) on low heat for 5 minutes. Add tomato wedges, mixing gently. Cook until tomatoes are heated thoroughly.

DeLane Dollinger
Venturia, North Dakota

Colorado Stir-Fry Ala Elk

Serves: 4
Prep Time: 30 minutes

1 **lb. elk, cut into thin strips**	½ **T. sugar**
cooking oil	2 **T. soy sauce**
½ **cup yellow onion, sliced**	2 **T. cornstarch**
1 **celery bunch, chopped**	¼ **cup mushrooms, sliced**
1 **cup bean sprouts**	
¼ **cup chestnuts, thinly sliced**	

In oil, stir-fry elk until cooked. Add vegetables (except mushrooms) and stir-fry for 2 minutes. Add seasonings and mushrooms and stir-fry for 3-5 minutes. Serve over hot rice.

Dion Luke
Glenwood Springs, Colorado

Elk Swiss Steak

Serves: 4
Prep Time: 20 minutes

2 **lbs. elk chuck steak**	1 **cup water**
flour	1 **small can whole tomatoes**
salt and pepper to taste	
parsley flakes to taste	3 **celery stalks, chopped**
garlic salt to taste	
1 **large onion, chopped**	

Cut meat into Swiss-steak-size pieces. Combine flour and seasonings and roll meat in mixture. Brown meat in oil, adding onions. Add water, tomatoes and celery. Pressure cook for 45 minutes. Use juice for gravy.

Jim Spielman
Ellington, Connecticut

Elk Chili

Serves: 4
Prep Time: 10 minutes

 2 lbs. ground elk
 **2 medium onions,
   chopped**
 **1 28-oz. can whole
   tomatoes**
 **1 16-oz. can kidney
   beans
   salt and pepper to taste
   chili powder to taste**

Brown meat and onions in 5-qt. saucepan. Add remaining
ingredients and simmer for 1 hour. Serve with crackers.

Jim Spielman
Ellington, Connecticut

Tender Elk Steak

Serves: 6
Prep Time: 2 hours

 **4-6 lbs. elk steak
   flour
   shortening**
 1 pkg. onion gravy mix
 **1 pkg. mushroom gravy
   mix
   salt and pepper to taste**

Coat steaks in flour. Brown steaks lightly on each side in
shortening. Place steaks in Dutch oven or baking dish. Mix both
gravy mixes in cold water according to directions. Pour gravy
mixture over steaks. Cover and bake in slow oven at 250-300
degrees for 1-2 hours.

Harry Wilkinson
Swisshome, Oregon

Elk Meatballs

Serves: 3-4
Prep Time: 1 hour, 30 minutes

1½ **lbs. elk**	1 **small onion, minced**
½ **cup oatmeal**	½ **cup milk**

Sauce:

1 **cup catsup**	3 **T. brown sugar**
1 **T. Worcestershire**	1 **cup water**
sauce	1 **T. vinegar**

Mix ingredients (except sauce) and form into small balls (about golf-ball size). Arrange in 9x12-inch pan. Combine ingredients for sauce and pour over balls. Bake at 350 degrees for 1 hour. (If doubling recipe, don't double vinegar.)

Charles Gay
Pierson, Florida

Wasatch Swiss Steak

Serves: 4-5
Prep Time: 6-7 hours

2 **lbs. elk steak**	1 **tsp. garlic powder**
½ **cup flour**	1½ **cups water**
3-4 **T. oil**	¾ **cup celery, chopped**
1 **T. Mrs. Dash**	3 **cups tomatoes**
seasoning	¾ **green pepper,**
1 **tsp. seasoning salt**	**chopped**
1 **tsp. pepper**	½ **lb. cheese**

Cut meat into serving-size pieces. Cover meat with flour and brown in hot oil. Remove meat and put in slow cooker. Blend remaining flour with hot drippings. Add seasonings. Blend in water and add vegetables. Cook and stir until thickened. Pour mixture over meat. Cook on low heat for 6-7 hours or until tender. Slice cheese. During last 5 minutes, put cheese on meat. Serve while hot.

Earl Leonhardt
West Jordan, Utah

Jackie's No-Name Casserole

Serves: 6
Prep Time: 45 minutes

2 lbs. ground elk
1 medium onion,
chopped
1 can tomatoes
1 can olives, sliced
1 tsp. garlic salt
¹/₄ tsp. oregano
6 tortillas
2-3 cups cheese, shredded
(any kind)

3 cups ready-cut
tomatoes
³/₄ green pepper, chopped
¹/₂ lb. cheese

Brown ground elk and onion. Add tomatoes, ³/₄ of olives, garlic salt and oregano. Cut tortillas into 1x4-inch strips. Layer ¹/₂ tortilla strips, ¹/₂ meat mixture, ¹/₂ cheese, repeat. Top with remaining olives. Bake at 350 degrees for 30 minutes.

Harry Wilkinson
Swisshome, Oregon

Crockpot Elk

Serves: 3-4
Prep Time: 30 minutes

2 large round elk steaks
1 large onion, chopped
1 bell pepper, chopped
1 qt. tomatoes
¹/₂ cup hot sauce
1 tsp. garlic powder
salt and pepper

Cut steaks into serving-size pieces. Place ingredients in layers in Crockpot. Cook for 10-12 hours.

Jack Bolick
Payson, Arizona

Hoffman's Moose Pizza

Serves: 3-4
Prep Time: 30 minutes

½ lb. ground moose
1 small onion, chopped
pizza dough
pizza sauce
3 oz. pepperoni
1 green pepper, chopped

Brown moose with onion. While meat is browning, prepare your favorite pizza dough. Shape dough in 14-inch round pizza pan. Cover dough with pizza sauce. Top with pepperoni, green pepper and other favorite toppings. Bake at 425 degrees for 20 minutes.

Sam Hoffman
Wright, Wyoming

Moose Roast

Serves: 2
Prep Time: 6 hours, 30 minutes

1 4-lb. moose roast
1 cup red wine
1 pkg. dry onion soup mix
salt to taste

Marinate meat in wine for at least 4 hours. Put meat in roasting bag or foil so it won't leak. Pour wine over meat. Put onion soup and salt on top. Bake at 325 degrees for 2 hours, 30 minutes or until tender.

Denise Reynoldson
Kimball, Nebraska

Moose Pot Roast

Serves: 2-4
Prep Time: overnight plus 2 hours, 15 minutes

1 6-lb. moose roast	**1 T. sugar**
½ tsp. curry powder	**3 onions, chopped**
1 tsp. salt	**2 celery stalks, chopped**
1 tsp. pepper	**2 T. flour**
½ tsp. thyme	**½ stick butter**

Put roast in pot and cover with water. Add curry powder, salt, pepper, thyme, sugar, onions and celery. Let soak overnight. Remove roast, cover it with flour and brown in butter. Add remaining ingredients to pot. Put roast in pot and cook at 350 degrees for about 2 hours.

Joe Depaolantonio
Colorado Springs, Colorado

Braised Sheep And Mushrooms

Serves: several
Prep Time: 1 hour

**2 lbs. sheep shoulder or
leg roast, sliced
flour
1 egg, beaten (with
small amount of milk)
2 cups crushed cereal
flakes
4 T. shortening
1 small can mushrooms**

Dip meat into flour, then into egg-and-milk mixture. Roll in finely crushed cereal flakes. Brown in hot shortening and cover with mushrooms and mushroom liquid. Cover and cook slowly until tender, about 45 minutes. Thicken liquid for gravy.

Robert Shenk
Columbia, Pennsylvania

Croquettes

Serves: 2
Prep Time: 20-30 minutes

>   **2 cups big-game meat
>   (any kind), minced
>   salt and pepper to taste
>   melted butter**
> **1½ eggs**
> **½ cup cracker crumbs or
>   bread crumbs**

Season meat and roll in butter to moisten. Then, mold meat into pear-shaped balls. Mix eggs and crumbs together. Dip meatballs into egg-crumb mixture. In butter, fry meatballs until brown. Serve.

Fred Van Haelst
Goodyear, Arizona

Bone Marrow

Serves: varies
Prep Time: 3 hours

>   **bones from big-game
>   animal (any kind)
>   flour
>   water**

Cover ends of bones with small pieces of plain dough (made with flour and water), securing by tying a floured cloth over dough. Place prepared bones upright in kettle and cover with boiling water. Boil for 2 hours. Remove cloth and push out marrow. Serve with dry toast.

Fred Van Haelst
Goodyear, Arizona

Brains And Eggs

Serves: varies
Prep Time: 30 minutes

> **brains (any game)**
> **bacon slices, finely**
> **chopped**
> **onion, finely chopped**
> **eggs, slightly beaten**
> **salt and pepper to taste**

Wash and clean brains. Dice meat into ½-inch cubes. Fry bacon and onion together until brown. Add diced brains and cook until nearly done. Then, add eggs and fry until scrambled. Season with salt and pepper.

Fred Van Haelst
Goodyear, Arizona

Tongue

Serves: 2
Prep Time: 3 hours

> **tongue (any big game)**
> **water**
> **mace**
> 1-2 **cloves**
> **Worcestershire sauce**
> **(optional)**

Soak tongue for 1 hour, then rinse in fresh water. Put tongue in kettle of cold water and bring to a boil. Then, skim and simmer for 2 hours or until tender. Add a blade of mace and cloves to improve gravy. Use Worcestershire sauce if desired.

Fred Van Haelst
Goodyear, Arizona

Corned Game

Serves: several
Prep Time: 4-6 days plus 3-4 hours

**whole shoulder or
shoulder roast (any big
game)
Morton's Tender Quick
your favorite vegetables**

Follow directions on back of Tender Quick bag for brine. Put roast and brine in oven roaster bag and refrigerate 4-6 days. Make sure entire roast is covered. When ready to cook, discard brine, rinse meat thoroughly, return meat to bag and cook for 2-3 hours at 300 degrees. Open bag and put in potatoes, carrots, onions, cabbage or whatever vegetables you like. Close bag and cook for 1 hour. Makes a great boiled dinner.

Dave Crowther
Bluemont, Virgina

Corned Wild Game

Serves: 2-3
Prep Time: 2 days plus 30 minutes

**5 lbs. meat (any kind)
6 T. salt
5 T. sugar (brown or
white)
1-2 tsp. salt
1 T. pepper**

Trim meat of all fat and sinew. Mix ingredients with enough water to cover meat. Let cure for 2 days. Wash meat several times in cold, clear water. Boil until tender. Serve with cooked cabbage (boiled or fried) with sliced onion.

Denise Reynoldson
Kimball, Nebraska

Wild Game Chili (Mild But Wild)

Serves: 4-6
Prep Time: 1 hour

- **2 lbs. ground big-game meat (any kind)**
- **butter**
- **1 tsp. salt**
- **1 tsp. pepper**
- **1 tsp. garlic powder**
- **1 large onion, chopped**
- **1 celery bunch, chopped**
- **2 15-oz. cans red kidney beans, undrained**
- **1 28-oz. can peeled tomatoes, undrained**
- **1 4-oz. can mushroom pieces and stems**
- **1 2-oz. jar Mexican chili seasoning powder**
- **2 shakes Mrs. Dash seasoning**
- **1 12-oz. can beer**

In frying pan, brown ground meat in butter. (Don't overcook.) Add salt, pepper and garlic powder to meat. Then, add onions and celery. Stir and saute until tender; drain grease. Add kidney beans, tomatoes, mushrooms and chili powder. Bring to a rapid boil for 5-10 minutes, stirring continuously. Lower heat and simmer for 30 minutes. Just before serving, add beer to pot and let stand for 5 minutes.

Steve Merrell
Pontiac, Michigan

Wild Game Ribs

Serves: 2-3
Prep Time: 2 hours

1 rack of ribs (any big game), cut into 3 parts

Spice mixture:	**1 T. garlic**
2 T. fresh parsley	**1½ tsp. salt**
2 T. fresh oregano	**1½ tsp. black pepper**
1½ tsp. fresh rosemary	**1 tsp. cayenne pepper**
1½ tsp. fresh thyme	

Place rib pieces on aluminum foil. Combine spice ingredients to form herb mixture. Rub spice mixture over surface of meat. Let stand at room temperature for 30-40 minutes. If using an open fire, let fire burn down to red coals. Wrap ribs in foil and lay on coals, or place on home barbecue grate. Cook for about 1 hour or until desired doneness. Serve with baked potatoes.

Dion Luke
Glenwood Springs, Colorado

Big Dave's Marinade Roast

Serves 4-6
Prep Time: 4 hours

1 front or hind quarter	**lemon pepper**
(any big game)	**1 lb. butter**
1 pkg. Heinz seasoning	**3-4 cabbage leaves**
½ cup water	**4-6 whole potatoes**
Season All salt	**1 onion, diced**

With fork, poke holes in thoroughly thawed roast. Mix Heinz seasoning with water and pour over meat. Sprinkle Season All salt and lemon pepper over entire portion. Spread butter on top of roast and cover completely with cabbage leaves. Add whole potatoes and onion around dish and cook at 350 degrees for 3-4 hours, basting every 30 minutes.

Dave Gutierrez
Stratford, Virginia

Wild Game Pastry

Serves: 2-4 depending on appetite
Prep Time: About 60 minutes

Pie Crust:
  3 cups flour
  ¹/₂ tsp. salt
  1 cup shortening
  ¹/₃ cup cold water

Filling:
1¹/₂ lbs. ground wild game
  6 medium sized
     potatoes, diced
  4 onions, diced
  1 tsp. black pepper
  2 tsp. salt

Combine flour and salt in large mixing bowl. (Traditional
Cornish recipe calls for white flour, but for variety try whole
wheat or other flours.) With pastry blender, or two table forks,
cut shortening into dry ingredients until mixture resembles fine
meal. Tablespoon by tablespoon, add cold water, mixing well.
Shape dough into several manageable size rounds and place in
tightly covered container. Then, refrigerate.

For filling: Combine vegetables, ground meat and salt and
pepper. Divide pastry and meat mixture each into four equal
portions. On a floured board, roll each portion of dough into
disk with 9-inch diameter. For each disk of dough, place a
portion of filling on ¹/₂ of disk. Moisten edge of disk with water
and fold unfilled half over to meet filled half. Crimp edges with
fork or twist with pastry rope to make a tight bond. Place in
shallow cookie pan and bake at 375 degrees for 30 minutes.
Reduce heat to 300 degrees and bake for 45 minutes more.
Pastries are best when served right from oven. Excellent when
served with mushroom gravy or covered with half-diluted
cream of mushroom soup.

Bill Miller
Chaska, Minnesota

Waterfowl

Grandpas, Dads & Decoys

by Bill Miller

The first hunting gear pieces I actually owned were a 20-gauge Remington 870 shotgun and a dozen mallard duck decoys. Prior to that, everything was hand-me-downs from one relative or another. Even the first shotgun I used for hunting was a 28-gauge Savage Stevens single shot that my dad bought for my mom before they were married. (That was back when he still had hopes of getting her hunting. Silly dad.)

Looking at the photos from my earliest hunting seasons, I can't help but smile. There I am holding my first rooster pheasant, kneeling next to my dad's dog and wearing one of his shrunken, discarded Indiana Jones-style hats. The shotgun and the vest were the hand-me-downs from mom, and two cousins (from separate families) contributed the bright plaid jacket and the rubber boots that were two sizes too big. The jeans were mine; no one older wore the dreaded "husky" sizes.

It sure was a treat to gather my own collection of huntin' stuff.

The 870 came like most first guns. It was one of those beautiful long, skinny boxes under the Christmas tree—the kind I still never tire of receiving. A few years earlier, I had been given a BB gun the same way. The lesson of that Christmas (a BB-sized dent in the living-room ceiling) made my dad all the wiser. There was no 20-gauge ammo in the house until after the initial excitement died down. When there was, it was carefully monitored and doled out only when we actually went shooting or hunting.

The decoys, on the other hand, were the first hunting gear I had to earn on my own. They were the result of a couple weeks' work helping my grandfather lay the stepping stones that created the sidewalk from the driveway to his house. Each individual 18x18-inch cement pad had to be cut into the sod to make a nice level sidewalk. And, boulders lurking below the lawn's surface had to be removed. Even in mid-July heat, Grandpa was a perfectionist.

There were 60 cement pads that had to be unloaded from the trailer, dug down, laid and leveled. Every five earned me one decoy of the $36 dozen.

Before we started the project, Grandpa and I selected the decoys out of Cabela's catalog. Then, we shook on the deal.

After getting married, my dad's waterfowl hunting was mostly jump shooting and pass shooting; so, I had never hunted with decoys before. As we looked at the catalog together, Grandpa told me about his early duck hunting days over crude cork decoys with hand-carved balsam heads. He had wonderful stories of how the ducks piled in on those simple, tattered dekes. Though I didn't realize it at the time, my grandfather was a master of motivation.

Every evening while listening to the ball games with my dad on the back porch, I read and reread the description of the Carry-Lite Aqua-keel magnums—the ones my 12-year-old mind was convinced worked better than any others ever built!

When the huge box finally arrived (several weeks after the project was complete), I went into hiding with my decoys. I took them out to the refurbished brooder coop which my brother and I called our club house and inspected each one over and over again. They were perfect!

For days, I laid my treasures on the grass each morning to mimic the decoy spreads recommended in the sporting magazines. Then, with my dad's springer spaniel Bingo sitting beside me, I'd squat next to a chokecherry tree in the front yard, imagining it was a flooded oak or cypress. I would blow grandpa's old black rubber duck call as loud and long as I could.

It drove my family nuts, but every day I took my limit of imaginary greenheads.

When setting spreads on the grass got old and I started thinking about actually going to the marsh to practice, I came to the sudden realization that I didn't have any anchors or anchor line for my decoys. Most of my summer's pay was laying at my feet, so there wasn't the option of asking Dad to stop at the hardware store. I needed all the money I had made by helping a neighbor bale hay. I had hidden it carefully in a jar under the floor of the clubhouse to buy the licenses I would need for the hunting seasons!

It didn't take me long to rescue a dozen lengths of used binder twine from the trash barrel in the barn. They were long enough, about the right marshy brown color and in infinite supply on the farm, so that took care of the anchor lines. But what about anchors?

Like most 12-year-olds, my mind didn't come up with simple solutions like rusty washers, discarded sections of lead pipe or even used horseshoes that were piled in a corner of the barn. No, these had to be special weights specifically made as anchors for my special decoys.

Dad humored me (probably just to see how far I'd take this), and picked up used tire weights at the local garage. At home, I grunted and groaned and pulled all the stubborn steel clips from the weights. Dad fired up his forge (left over from the days when he used to shoe his own horses), and melted down the scrap lead.

He showed me how to make wet sand moulds, and we cast some mighty stout anchors, each with a large size fence staple for attaching the anchor line. My decoys wouldn't move in a hurricane with these mega-anchors in place.

I've still got the decoys; still use 'em. I still have a few of the anchors, too, though they are relegated to the garage these days. (Some weigh close to a pound and there's no way to keep 'em from tangling.) The 870 shotgun was traded long ago for "somethin' better."

Guess that shows the difference between what we're given and what we earn.

Roast Duck With Stuffing

Serves: 4-6
Prep Time: 2 hours, 30 minutes

  2 **ducks, cleaned and dressed**
1¹/₂ **tsp. salt**
 ³/₈ **tsp. pepper**
 ¹/₄ **cup melted butter**
2-3 **T. lemon juice (or lime)**

Stuffing:

¹/₂ **cup carrots, grated**
¹/₂ **cup yellow onion, chopped**
¹/₂ **cup celery, chopped**
2-3 **T. celery leaves, chopped**
¹/₂ **cup apples, cored and chopped**
¹/₂ **cup butter, melted**
¹/₂ **tsp. salt**
dash of fresh ground pepper

¹/₂ **tsp. thyme**
  1 **qt. dry bread crumbs or cubes**
³/₄ **cup giblet stock, bouillon or white wine**

Preheat oven to 325 degrees. Dry ducks inside and out. Rub salt and pepper on inside of ducks. Combine melted butter and lemon juice. Brush butter mixture on inside and outside of ducks. Stuff and truss ducks. Wrap ducks in aluminum foil and place in shallow roasting pan. Bake in slow oven for 1 hour, 30 minutes. Remove foil and baste with pan drippings. Bake and baste 30 minutes until meat is a rich brown color. For stuffing, saute vegetables and apple in butter until tender. Add seasonings to bread crumbs. Toss. Add sauteed vegetables and toss once more. Add stock to moisten. (Recipe for stuffing can be doubled.) Put half of dressing in ducks and serve remaining as side dish. If dry, drizzle with stock.

Walter Squier
Portland, Connecticut

Marinated Duck Breasts With Homefried Potatoes & Onion

Serves: 4-8
Prep Time: overnight plus 30 minutes

8 duck breasts, sliced
¼ qt. beer
1 cup red wine
salt and pepper to taste
1 garlic clove, pressed

4 large potatoes, chunked
1 large onion, chunked
1 stick margarine

Marinate breasts overnight in beer, wine, salt and pepper and garlic. In large skillet, cook potatoes in margarine until browned. Add onions and more margarine as needed until onions are translucent. Fry meat in margarine or oil until done. Serve with garden salad.

Dick Greeno
Lowell, Massachusetts

Quick Tender Ducks By Pressure Cooker

Serves: 4-6
Prep Time: 1 hour

4 ducks
1 onion, grated
1 garlic clove, minced
other favorite
vegetables and spices
1 cup orange juice

In 6-qt. pressure cooker (fits 4 ducks vertically), combine vegetables. Then, add birds and juice. Seal cooker and bring to 15 lbs. for 28 minutes. Take off stove and let pressure go down. Serve. If wanted browned, take ducks out with 2 forks (otherwise birds will fall apart) and place in roasting pan with some juice. Add bacon strips across each duck and put in oven at 425 degrees. Bake until ducks are browned as desired.

Edmond Leahy
San Francisco, California

Duck And Sausage Gumbo

Serves: 4-6
Prep Time: 1 hour

3 mallard ducks	**1 cup celery, chopped**
1 cup olive oil	**2 lbs. fresh pork sausage**
1 cup flour	**1 cup green onion and**
3 cups onions, chopped	**parsley, minced**
1 cup green pepper,	**salt, black and cayenne**
chopped	**pepper to taste**

Make dark roux by heating oil in skillet and adding flour. Stir continuously until flour is chocolate brown. Add onions, celery and green pepper. Cook until vegetables are tender. Par boil ducks in pot. Bone ducks and reserve stock. Fry smoked sausage. Put sausage in roux and add stock from ducks. Add ducks. Add more water if needed to fill pot. Cover and simmer for 1 hour. Add water and simmer another 30 minutes. Add green onions and parsley. Season with spices to taste. Turn fire off; cover and let stand without heat.

Robert Bisso
Memphis, Tennessee

Duck Filet Mignon

Serves: 2-4
Prep Time: overnight plus 5 minutes

2 duck breasts	**Heinz 57 sauce**
toothpicks	**bacon**
sealable plastic bags	**barbecue sauce**

Fillet breast meat. Cut fillets into 2x2-inch cubes. Place cubes in sealable plastic bags, adding Heinz 57 sauce as marinade. Cover cubes completely and place bags in refrigerator overnight. Then, remove cubes and place bacon around them, securing with toothpicks. Place cubes on grill for approximately 3 minutes. (Time may vary.)

Peter Burke
Modesto, California

Duck Dressed To Kill

Serves: 4-6
Prep Time: 2 hours

- **1 1¼-lb. duck, fresh or frozen**
- **2 large apples**
- **1 small onion, thinly sliced**
- **½ tsp. caraway seeds**
- **1 16-oz. can sauerkraut**
- **3 T. butter or olive oil**
- **⅛ tsp. garlic powder**
- **1 T. parsley**
  pearl onions
  baby peas
  baby carrots
  parsley

If fresh, rinse and dry duck. If frozen, thaw, rinse and dry duck. Combine ½ apple, cored and shredded (skin on), with some onion, a sprinkle of caraway seed and ⅓ to ½ cup sauerkraut. Stuff mixture into duck cavity. Truss Legs. In shallow roaster, place duck breast-side up. Brush olive oil over entire duck. Season with garlic powder. Roast (uncovered) at 350 degrees for 2 hours. Check after 1 hour, 30 minutes with meat thermometer in thigh area for 180 degrees. If bird is browned, cover with foil after 1 hour, 30 minutes. Saute rest of onion in remaining oil. Add remaining apples, cored and shredded. Add rest of caraway seeds, parsley and sauerkraut; heat thoroughly. Remove duck when done. Let sit 5 minutes. On platter, arrange prepared pearl onions, baby peas and baby carrots around edge. Put sauerkraut in center. Lay duck on sauerkraut. Garnish with parsley at bow and stern. Serve with homemade biscuits.

Walter Squier
Portland, Connecticut

BBQ Duck

Serves: 2-3
Prep Time: 30 minutes

1 duck	**2 tsp. prepared mustard**
salt	**1 tsp. Worcestershire**
paprika	**sauce**
1/8 cup water	**1 T. butter**

Cut whole breast (bone in) from duck, with or without skin. Broil breasts for 10 minutes or until browned. Season with salt and paprika. While breasts are browning, combine remaining ingredients. Let mixture warm slowly so butter melts without burning. (Do not put over direct heat.) Broil breasts 10 more minutes, basting with sauce.

Gerald Foldenauer
King Cove, Alaska

Uncle Rod's Smoked Snow Goose

Serves: 4-10 or more
Prep Time: 3-5 days plus 6-8 hours

2-10 snow goose breasts	**oregano flakes**
salt	**garlic powder**
brown sugar	**basil flakes**
crushed red pepper	**honey**
black pepper	

Skin and fillet goose breasts. Put breasts in pan of saltwater. In 6-qt. kettle, layer bottom with above ingredients (except honey). Put a layer of condiments, then layer of breasts ... until all breasts are in pot and covered with ingredients. Cover pot and refrigerate for 3-5 days. Stir mixture once a day after the first 24 hours. (It makes a thick briny soup on the 3rd and 5th day.) Heat a Weber kettle with coals in the middle. Put foil with chips inside (that have soaked for a day) on coals. Put breasts around outside of grill. Cover and smoke 6-8 hours. Brush breasts with honey.

Rod Williamson
Modesto, California

Jim's Goose Curry

Serves: 4
Prep Time: 30 minutes

2-4 cups breast meat, broiled and cubed	**1 8-oz. can water chestnuts, drained**
¼ cup onion, chopped	**1 tsp. curry powder**
1 green pepper, chopped	**1 tsp. ginger**
2 T. butter or margarine	**½ tsp. salt**
1½ cups water	**½ tsp. pepper**
1 8-oz. can tomato sauce	**1 tsp. garlic powder**
1 4-oz. can mushrooms	**2 T. cornstarch**
	¼ cup water

Saute onion and green pepper in butter. Blend in remaining ingredients (except cornstarch and water). Cook until heated thoroughly, stirring occasionally. Combine cornstarch and water. Add cornstarch mixture to ingredients to obtain desired thickness. Serve over rice or noodles.

Jim Loper
Gilchrist, Oregon

Pa's Game Breast

Serves: 6
Prep Time: 1 hour, 30 minutes

2 whole goose breasts, boned	**½ pt. sour cream**
½ lb. chipped beef	**1 10 ½-oz. can cream of mushroom soup**
6 bacon strips, fried crisp and diced	**1 cup mushrooms**

Cut goose breasts into bite-sized chunks and arrange on bottom of greased pan. Sprinkle shredded chipped beef over breasts. Top breasts with bacon pieces. Combine sour cream and soup. Spread soup mixture over breasts in baking dish. Top with mushrooms. Cover and bake at 350 degrees for 1 hour or until done.

John Burke
Philadelphia, Pennsylvania

Chestnut & Liver Stuffing For Wild Goose

Serves: 6-10
Prep Time: 1 hour

1 goose liver	**2 cups bread crumbs**
2 lbs. chestnuts	**3 T. parsley, chopped**
2 cups stock	**½ lemon rind, grated**
2 T. butter	**½ T. thyme**
4 apples	**½ T. marjoram**
1 large onion, chopped	**salt and pepper to taste**

Boil chestnuts in water for about 5 minutes until both outer shell and inner skin can be removed. Cover nuts with stock and simmer until tender. Drain (reserve stock) and let cool. Saute liver in butter until firm and then chop. Peel and chop apples and mix with onion. Saute in butter for about 3 minutes. Add chestnuts, liver, bread crumbs, parsley, lemon rind, and seasonings. Mix together with enough stock to make stuffing moist, but firm. Stuff goose and close. Remember to add 20-25 minutes to the cooking time if goose is stuffed.

Mike Vail
Plymouth, Minnesota

Fruit & Honey-Glazed Honker

Serves: 4
Prep Time: 2 hours

1 goose	**½ cup honey**
apple or potato	**1 T. brandy**
1 cup preserves	**1 T. orange liqueur**

Put peeled apple or potato inside goose to absorb strong flavors while cooking. Prick goose all over. Bake at 350 degrees, allowing 20-25 minutes per pound for a small goose; 15 minutes for larger bird. Combine remaining ingredients. Remove goose about 20 minutes before done and coat with glaze mixture. Bake until glaze has caramelized.

Kari Wasson
Frontenac, Minnesota

Chuck's Goose Spaghetti

Serves: 4
Prep Time: 1 hour, 15 minutes

breasts from 2 geese	**1 large onion**
1 box Kraft Tangy	**garlic powder**
Italian Spaghetti	**freshly ground pepper**
2 15-oz. cans	**2 4-oz. cans mushrooms**
tomato sauce	

Dice goose breasts and yellow onion in large frying pan.
Season meat with garlic powder and pepper. Add package of
seasoning from mix. Heat and stir until all onions are clear. Add
cans of tomato sauce and drained mushrooms. Simmer for 1
hour. Prepare pasta and pour sauce over it to serve.

Chuck Barry
Houston, Texas

Gourmet Goose Salad

Serves: 4
Prep Time: 15 minutes

1 leftover roast goose,	**2 carrots, chopped**
shredded	**2 celery stalks, chopped**
mayonnaise	**2 hardboiled eggs,**
3 tsp. lemon juice	**chopped**
2 tsp. yellow prepared	**4 tomatoes, top sliced**
mustard	**off and hollowed out**
dash of Tabasco sauce	**salt and pepper**
macaroni	

Put goose meat into large mixing bowl. Add enough
mayonnaise to moisten well. Add lemon juice, mustard and
dash of Tabasco sauce. Mix well. Add carrots, celery, eggs
and cooked, drained and cooled macaroni, then mix lightly.
Season with salt and pepper to taste. Spoon into hollowed out
tomatoes and serve as light lunch.

Bill Miller
Chaska, Minnesota

You'll Never Guess It's Goose

Serves: 4
Prep Time: 1 hour, 30 minutes

3 goose breasts, boned	**1 can mushrooms**
3 eggs, beaten	**Muenster cheese**
Italian bread crumbs	**slices**
1 stick margarine	**1 can beef broth**
½ fresh lemon	

Cut goose breasts into chunks and soak in beaten eggs for 20 minutes. Roll meat in bread crumbs and brown in margarine. Place in 9x13-inch casserole. Squeeze lemon over meat. Sprinkle with mushrooms; layer with cheese slices. Pour broth over all and cover with foil. Bake at 350 degrees for 1 hour.

Kermit Skelton
Raleigh, North Carolina

Goose On The Grill

Serves: 4
Prep Time: overnight plus 1 hour

2 wild goose breasts,
**   boned**
1 cup lemon juice
1 shot Tabasco sauce
2 tsp. salt
1 onion, finely diced
**   seasoned salt**
**   pepper**
**   margarine, melted**

Marinate goose breasts overnight in mixture of lemon juice, Tabasco sauce, salt and onion. Cook drained breasts over medium heat on grill; cook until medium rare. During cooking, baste with melted margarine and season with seasoned salt and pepper. Serve with baked potato and greens.

Mike Boeselager
Maribel, Wisconsin

Grilled Coot

Serves: 4
Prep Time: 15-35 minutes

- **4 whole coots (leave skin on)**
- **charcoal briquettes**
- **1 whole lemon, quartered**
- **olive oil**
- **salt and pepper**
- **8 whole juniper berries**
- **4 celery tops (with leaves)**
- **4 small potatoes**
- **4 small white onions**

Start charcoal briquettes in grill. Pat cavities and outside of coots dry with paper towels. Rub each coot cavity with one lemon quarter, then with olive oil. Set aside lemon quarters. Season cavity with salt and pepper. Inside each cavity, place 2 juniper berries, 1 celery top, 1 potato and 1 onion. Tie drumsticks across cavity with wet kitchen string. Tuck wing tips behind back. Rub outside of each coot with lemon quarter, then with olive oil. Season with salt and pepper. When charcoal briquettes are covered with ash, spread them evenly in grill. Place grate above hot coals. Grill coots until desired doneness, turning once or twice and brushing with olive oil.

Robert Shenk
Columbia, Pennsylvania

Small Game

Rabbit Hunters

by Dr. John Woods

Over my years of closely observing the subspecies of humans known as hunters, I've developed the theory that there truly exists two separate, but equal breeds of rabbit hunters here in the South. They're both all-American, but they are as different as mallards and bobwhite quail.

Every Southern rabbit hunter falls into one of these categories, maybe even both at times. However, each hunter is likely to show strong tendencies of one breed type over the other. Anyway, that's how it appears to this casual, sideline observer of Southern traditions, either real or imagined.

The breeds referred to are known by several names below the Mason-Dixon line. Most likely there might be some more localized nicknames that also apply. Basically, we are talking about the Meat Hunters (or Gun Hunters, depending on who you're talking to) and the Dog Chasers. This latter group might also be called the Houndsmen in a loose sense of the word.

Both groups are true-blooded American Southern rabbit hunters to the core, but their goals (and behaviors) afield differ considerably (as well as off the field, come to think of it).

You can spot a meat or gun hunter immediately, because he is rarely separated from his shooting iron. He totes a heavy load of shotshells in looped belts or in his sagging hunting coat. If bandaleros were in good taste for hunters, this guy would be sure to wear them.

Attached to his already overloaded coat is a game bag plenty large enough to handle a day's limit of cottontails, and then some.

The meat hunter wears leather hunting boots, and lighter-weight brush pants, never chaps. He fully intends for the dogs to bring the quarry well within reasonable shooting range. He tries to avoid all brambles and waist-deep thornbushes, because after all, who could shoot a running rabbit in that mess anyway.

The meat hunter's only interest where rabbit dogs are concerned is in terms of pure production. The measure of success is in the weight of his game bag at the hunt's end. Dogs are simply a means to an end for the meat hunter.

The meat hunter will spend copious time bending the ears of his hunting partners, and anyone who'll listen for that matter, explaining the great and difficult shots he made that day. Hours will be spent pouring over all the grisly details of the ones that got away, and which dog allowed the escape. After the hunt, talk about history's greatest rabbit guns will also prevail.

Very little will be said about the dog's grand effort in the field by the meat hunter, unless of course he should limit out in record time. Usually though, the dogs are quickly boxed so they aren't in the way when the discussion turns to more important things like the ideal shotgun barrel length, custom choking of rabbit guns or the merits of magnum loads. Talk of missed shots is strictly forbidden.

Now, on the other side of the spectrum of Southern rabbit hunters are the houndsmen or dog chasers. Again, these "gentlemen" hunters can be as easily identified as the meat hunters. They seldom carry rabbit guns. Instead, they are often seen with dog-handling leashes of leather and chain, enough to restrain a huge pack at ankle's length.

A dog chaser's gear afield differs greatly from the meat hunter's. Many dog chasers somehow feel that they are compelled to follow each dog into the bush regardless of the pace or the cover's thickness. Hence, the wearing of armor-plated, brush-busting pants is of the highest order. Some smart clothing manufacturer is going to make a fortune off these guys someday by inventing a lightweight suit of armor.

Most often, you'll find the true champions of this breed garbed from head to toe in Filson clothing—double layered "tin cloth" no less. Even so, it is chronically tattered beyond recognition, yet holding its own. Their boots will repel mud, water and snakes in the infested jungles they encounter in pursuit of their trumpeting canines. Some of the more relaxed dog chasers will carry the optional walking stick, or maybe a whittling knife and a beagling horn. (That's right, a *beagling* not *bugling* horn!)

Most times, the houndsmen can be seen afield with at least one hand cupped around their best ear. Like miniature radar stations, they try to keep honed-in on the frequency of their dogs in the chase. Regardless of the total number of hounds in the pack, the true dog chaser can recite the name of each one as they bellow and cry. The best can even tell you how the dog is feeling that day. Of course, it doesn't matter if they name them incorrectly or are incorrect about the dog's inclination because the other hunters don't know each others' dogs anyway!

Dog chasers exhibit the keenest respect for the care and handling of their hounds. More money, time and effort will be spent in maintaining decent dog boxes than the vehicles they reside in. They take great pride in the fact that a single, condominium dog box can handle 10 to 15 hounds with no problems.

The dogs themselves are always well fed, and each sports an

individualized and personalized collar. The data that can be squeezed onto a dog collar nameplate would amaze anyone. The standard information will include the owner's name, address, phone number, social security number, place of employment, number of children, the dog's feeding preferences and oh, yes, the dog's name ... maybe. Veteran dog men know that the surest way to lose a successful hound is for a suspicious stranger to know the pup's name!

Some dog chasers have even been known to subscribe to a worldwide dog search network complete with a toll-free, call-in number to help recover dogs lost during a hunt. Such dogs wear special collars that can be tracked via satellite. A dog found without such a collar surely belongs to a meat hunter.

Both breeds of rabbit hunters are indeed true sportsmen. They are not even opposed to each other. In fact, some of the best rabbit hunts to experience are when the two groups are virtually in equal force in the field at the same time.

Meat hunters and dog chasers get along just fine. After all, the bottom line is the enjoyment of the great outdoors and the free-spirited pursuit of one's favorite hunting sport. It can be connecting on a difficult shot at a speeding swamper, or just trekking the landscape while listening to "Little Chipper" mouth away on a hot trail.

It makes little difference in the final analysis which classified breed of official rabbit hunter someone belongs to, as long as they enjoy the sport, teach a few newcomers about the enjoyment and work to make sure future generations have the same pleasures down the road.

After all, neither breed of Southern rabbit hunter would turn down a steaming plate of rabbit stew, some hot biscuits, maybe a side of grits, and, of course, a healthy slice of "Pee-Can" pie to polish off the deal.

Braised Rabbit

Serves: 2
Prep Time: 1 hour

1 **rabbit, cut up**	1 **large onion, chopped**
cooking oil	2 **cups water**
2 **carrots, chopped**	**chicken bouillon**
2 **celery stalks, chopped**	**pepper to taste**
2 **potatoes, chopped**	**cornstarch**

In small amount of oil, saute rabbit until browned. Remove meat to casserole dish. Place vegetables around rabbit. Pour in water. Cover with lid and bake at 325 degrees until tender. When all is tender, remove to serving dishes. In remaining liquid, stir in bouillon and pepper. Add enough water to make 2 cups of liquid. Make a solution of ½ cup water and 2 T. cornstarch and stir into boiling liquid to make gravy.

Robert Gailey
Nezperce, Idaho

Jim's Best Bunnies

Serves: 4
Prep Time: 1 hour, 15 minutes

2 **rabbits, cut up**	3 **carrots, chunked**
6 **bacon slices**	2 **celery stalks, chunked**
cooking oil	½ **cup onions, chopped**
2 **medium onions,**	1½ **T. parsley, chopped**
quartered	1 **tsp. thyme**
1 **garlic clove, pressed**	2 **cups dry red wine**

In cast-iron Dutch oven, fry bacon until crisp. Remove and save. In cooking oil, saute onion and garlic until transparent. Remove onion and garlic and discard. Brown rabbit on all sides in remaining oil. When all of rabbit is browned, add remaining ingredients and bring to a boil. Remove from heat and crumble bacon on top. Bake (covered) at 350 degrees for 1 hour. Serve with rice.

Jim Demilio
Spring Lake, Michigan

Pork Bunny

Serves: 4-6
Prep Time: 30 minutes

2-3 medium rabbits, cut up
  1 lb. bacon strips
  1 small bottle red wine
     or cooking sherry
  1 12-oz. bottle barbecue
     sauce

Lay rabbits in 9x13-inch cake pan. Criss-cross bacon strips on rabbit sections. (Use toothpicks to secure bacon.) Saute in red wine or sherry. Brush with barbecue sauce. Bake at 300 degrees (covered with tinfoil) for about 45 minutes or more, depending on oven. Baste occasionally with barbecue sauce and wine or sherry.

Raymond Phillips Jr.
Escanaba, Michigan

Rabbit Casserole

Serves: 6
Prep Time: 2 hours

4 rabbits, cooked
1 small can sliced
   carrots
1 small can peas
1 small can diced
   potatoes
1 can sliced mushrooms

1 onion, chopped
8 oz. egg noodles,
   cooked
   salt and pepper to taste
4 packets brown gravy
   mix

Cut meat into small pieces and place in large casserole dish. Add all ingredients (except gravy mix). Prepare gravy according to package directions. (Should make approximately 2 cups.) Pour gravy over mixture. Toss lightly. Bake for 1 hour at 350 degrees.

Kirby Brought
Middleburg, Pennsylvania

Suzy Q's Wabbit Egg Wolls

Serves: 25-30 large egg rolls
Prep Time: 1 hour, 45 minutes

1 large rabbit	**1 small can mushrooms**
1 cup margarine	**1 small can bean sprouts**
1 bowl green onions,	**¹/₂ tsp. salt**
chopped	**¹/₂ tsp. garlic salt**
¹/₂ cabbage head,	**2 pkgs. egg roll shells**
shredded	**1 egg, beaten**

Boil rabbit until tender (about 1 hour), cook and bone. In large skillet, melt margarine. Saute onions, cabbage, drained mushrooms and sprouts until tender. Add rabbit, salt and garlic salt. Chill for 30 minutes. Put 2 T. of mixture into shell, roll and brush with egg. Fry until golden brown. Tastes great with soy sauce and hot mustard!

Mike and Suzy Q Moore
Huffman, Texas

Sour Sweet Rabbit

Serves: 4
Prep Time: 30 minutes

2 rabbits	**1 T. soy sauce**
flour	**¹/₄ cup vinegar**
butter	**¹/₂ cup sugar**
1 8-oz. can pineapple	**salt to taste**
rings, reserve juice	**1 bell pepper, sliced**
¹/₄ cup catsup	

Cut rabbit into bite-sized pieces, coat with flour and saute in butter. Place meat in casserole dish. Pour pineapple juice over meat. Mix catsup, soy sauce, vinegar, sugar and salt. Place pineapple rings and bell pepper slices on meat. Pour above mixture over all and simmer until tender.

Donald McIntyre
Pleasantville, Pennsylvania

Jack Rabbit Chili

Serves: 2-3
Prep Time: 1 hour, 30 minutes

1½ lbs. ground rabbit
1 lb. ground beef
(optional)
1 medium onion,
chopped
½ red onion, chopped
1 bell pepper, chopped
2 cans whole tomatoes
(in own juice)
1-2 15½-oz. cans chili
beans
1-2 15½-oz. cans kidney
beans
1 cup red wine
1 T. Worcestershire
sauce
1 T. soy sauce
1 6-oz. can tomato paste
2 bay leafs
1 tsp. dry mustard
2-3 tsp. chili powder
1 tsp. pepper
½ tsp. garlic salt
½ tsp. oregano
¼ tsp. red pepper

Brown meat, onions and green bell pepper. Drain. Combine all other ingredients in pot. Add meat, onions and bell pepper. Simmer for at least 1 hour.

James Hendricks
Lakeside, California

East Texas Rabbit Chili

Serves: 6
Prep Time: 3-4 hours

- 1 **large rabbit**
- ½ **tsp. garlic salt**
- 1 **tsp. black pepper**
- ½ **lb. pork sausage**
- 1 **medium onion,**
  chopped
- 1 **tsp. oregano**
- 1 **tsp. curry powder**
- 1 **15-oz. can ranch-style**
  beans
- 1 **tsp. cayenne pepper**
- 1 **T. cumin**
- 3 **T. chili powder**
- 3 **8-oz. cans tomato**
  sauce
- 1 **cup water**

Cut rabbit meat into small chunks. Sprinkle garlic salt and black pepper on rabbit. In large skillet, combine pork sausage, rabbit, onion, oregano, curry powder and cayenne pepper. Cook until brown. Drain drippings from meat. Remove meat mixture into large pot and combine all remaining ingredients. Bring to a boil. Then, simmer for 3-4 hours (covered). Add more cayenne pepper and chili powder if too mild.

Neil Means
Spurger, Texas

Rabbit On A Shingle

Serves: 4
Prep Time: 40 minutes

1 **rabbit, cut up**	1 **can or jar of gravy**
salt and pepper	4 **Swiss cheese slices**
1½ **cups flour**	1-2 **onions, sliced**
½ **cup cooking oil**	**(optional)**
4 **bread slices**	

Season rabbit with salt and pepper. Put flour in large bowl and dredge rabbit pieces generously. Then, brown rabbit in cooking oil over medium heat. Place bread slices on plates. On stove, heat gravy in small pan. Slice rabbit meat off bone and place on bread slices. Add gravy, cheese slices and onion. Serve while warm.

Samuel Mears
Onancock, Virginia

Emma's Alabama Rabbit Stew

Serves: 5
Prep Time: 1 hour, 30 minutes

5-7 **rabbits**	2 **T. sugar**
2 **cans tomatoes**	**dash of hot pepper**
1 **small can tomato paste**	**salt and pepper to taste**
6 **cups potatoes, diced**	1 **can cream-style corn**
2 **cups onions, chopped**	
½ **tsp. Worcestershire**	
sauce	
1 **garlic clove, minced**	
1 **T. celery salt**	

Cook rabbits in water. Remove bones. Add all ingredients (except corn). Cook until potatoes are done. Add corn and enough water to make 7 quarts. Boil a few minutes longer and serve.

Fritz Behrens
Anderson, Indiana

Grilled Marinated Rabbit

Serves: 2
Prep Time: 24-36 hours

**1 medium-large rabbit,
  quartered**
**1 cup white wine
  vinegar**
2 cups soy oil
2 cups white wine
2 bay leaves
1 onion, thickly chopped

4 garlic cloves, crushed
**1 T. whole black
  peppercorns**
1 T. salt
2 celery tops (leaves)
**2 fresh rosemary sprigs
  (optional)**

Combine all ingredients and whisk together. Add rabbit parts
and let marinate 1-2 days. Grill rabbit, turning every 4-5
minutes until done. Use marinade to brush on rabbit while
grilling. (This marinade is good for 6 weeks when refrigerated.)

James Distel
Philadelphia, Pennsylvania

Stew With Dumplings

Serves: 2
Prep Time: 1 hour

**1 whole squirrel
  water**
1 pod red hot pepper

salt and pepper
**1 small pkg. canned
  biscuits**

Dress squirrel. Clean and boil in pot with water, red hot pepper
and salt and pepper. Boil until done and tender. Tear squirrel
apart with fingers. Tear canned biscuits into small pieces. Put
squirrel pieces and biscuit pieces back in boiling water and
pepper. Cook until dumplings are done. Serve with dry red
wine and Georgia rice.

Edward Hargett
Columbus, Georgia

Bushy Tail Stew

Serves: 4-6
Prep Time: 2 hours, 15 minutes

6 gray squirrels	**3 tomatoes, cubed**
1 12-oz. can chicken	**1 green pepper, cubed**
gravy	**1 can cream-style corn**
4 qts. water	**1 can yellow-eye beans**
12 oz. bacon, cooked and	**1 T. salt**
crumbled	**2 T. cornstarch**
1 onion, cubed	**1 cup milk**

Boil squirrels in chicken gravy and water for 1 hour. Remove all bones and strain liquid. To the liquid, add bacon, onion, tomatoes, peppers, corn, beans and salt. Boil for 30 minutes. While boiling, cut squirrel into bite-sized pieces, add to stew and boil 30 minutes longer, stirring constantly. Before serving, pour in cornstarch and milk until thickened.

Roger Plouff
Cape Neddick, Maine

Baked Gray Squirrel

Serves: 4
Prep Time: 1 hour, 30 minutes

4 squirrels, cut up
1 cup flour
1/2 tsp. salt
1 egg, beaten
cooking oil
1 1/2 cups water

Thoroughly wash squirrel. Combine flour and salt in plastic bag. Dip squirrel meat in beaten egg, then place in bag. Shake to coat meat evenly. Fry meat in hot cooking oil, browning on both sides. Drain oil from pan and add water. Cover meat and place in oven. Bake at 350 degrees for 1 hour or until meat is tender.

John Spryszak
Falls Creek, Pennsylvania

Succulent Squirrel

Serves: 4
Prep Time: 1-2 hours

4 **squirrels, dressed**	**pinch of paprika**
1 **16-oz. bottle zesty**	**pinch of ground sage**
Italian dressing	**salt and pepper to taste**
8 **small potatoes, sliced**	4 **T. bacon bits**
2 **onions, sliced**	4 **T. barbecue sauce**
pinch of celery seed	4-6 **carrots, sliced**

In refrigerator, soak dressed squirrels overnight in saltwater mixture. Rinse off with fresh water and place on backs in deep cake pan. Pour Italian dressing over meat and marinate for 4-6 hours. Place layer of potatoes and onions in aluminum foil. Lay squirrel on top on its back. Add spices to suit taste including bacon bits and barbecue sauce. Place carrots inside body cavity and another layer of potatoes and onions on top, wrapping completely with foil. Repeat with remaining squirrels.

Rev. Kenneth White
Brandenburg, Kentucky

Fricasseed Squirrel

Serves: 3-4
Prep Time: 15-20 minutes

3 **squirrels, cut up**	1 **cup meat bouillon**
1/2 **tsp. salt**	3 **bacon slices, minced**
1/4 **tsp. pepper**	2 **tsp. lemon juice**
1/4 **cup flour**	1 **celery stalk with leaves**
cooking oil	1/2 **tsp. thyme**

Rub squirrel pieces with salt and pepper and roll in flour. In heavy skillet, fry meat in cooking oil with bacon pieces until brown on all sides. Add remaining ingredients. Cover and simmer for 1 hour until tender. Serve with rice or noodles.

Ronald Overly
Minot, North Dakota

Squirrel And Gravy

Serves: 2-4
Prep Time: 45 minutes

2 squirrels	**flour**
garlic powder to taste	**1/3 cup shortening**
salt and pepper to taste	**2 cups milk**

Cut each leg of squirrel off, and halve the backs. Add garlic powder and salt and pepper. Roll meat in flour and brown pieces in shortening. Take drippings and add an equal amount of flour. Add milk, stir and cook over medium heat to desired thickness. Serve gravy with squirrel over mashed potatoes, or over bread.

Eric Grove
Nappanee, Indiana

Squirrel Au Vin

Serves: 2-4
Prep Time: 3 hours, 30 minutes

2 squirrels, cut up	**1/2 lb. mushrooms, sliced**
1/2 cup flour	**4-6 carrots, cut in halves**
1 tsp. salt	**lengthwise**
1/4 tsp. pepper	**1 cup chicken broth**
6 bacon slices	**1 cup red burgundy wine**
2 large onions, thinly	**1/2 tsp. garlic chips**
sliced	**1/2 tsp. salt**

Coat squirrels with seasoned flour (flour, salt and pepper). In large skillet or Dutch oven, fry bacon until crisp; then, remove and drain meat. Brown squirrel and set aside. Add onions and mushrooms to pan, and cook until onions are tender. Put squirrel back into pan. Crumble bacon and add remaining ingredients. Cover and simmer for 2-3 hours or until squirrel is tender.

Carl Runke
Hutchinson, Minnesota

Russ's Sauteed Squirrel

Serves: 2-3
Prep Time: 1 hour

  2 squirrels, cut up
2-3 T. butter
     Worcestershire sauce
  2 tsp. white wine
     salt and pepper
     seasonings to taste

Melt butter in pan. Add squirrel, Worcestershire sauce and
wine. Turn meat every 15 minutes, cooking each side twice.
Add seasonings to taste.

Russ Bolton
Griffin, Georgia

Fried Squirrel

Serves: 3
Prep Time: 1-2 hours

  4 squirrels
 ½ onion, chopped
     vegetable flakes
     flour
     butter or cooking oil
     salt and pepper to taste

Boil squirrels in large pot of water. Add onion and vegetable
flakes. Boil for about 1 hour, 15 minutes (covered). Remove
squirrel and discard water. Brush small amount of melted butter
or cooking oil on each squirrel. Mix a little salt and pepper in
flour. Cover each squirrel with mixture. Fry squirrel on each
side until brown, about 10 minutes.

John Smith
Fayetteville, Pennsylvania

Carl's Squirrels

Serves: varies
Prep Time: 4 hours, 30 minutes

squirrels, cut up	**soda crackers, ground**
½ cup vinegar	**corn oil**
cornflakes, ground	

Soak squirrel pieces in saltwater and vinegar for 4 hours or overnight; rinse. Boil meat until tender; dry. Put meat in bag with ground cornflakes and soda crackers and shake. Fry in corn oil at 375 degrees until browned.

Carl Runke
Hutchinson, Minnesota

Squirrel And Rabbit Dumplings

Serves: 4-6
Prep Time: 1 hour, 30 minutes

1 medium rabbit	**½ tsp. salt**
3 small squirrels	**½ cup onion, chopped**
water	

Dumplings:	**½ cup lard**
2 cups flour	**½ cup butter or**
½ tsp. salt	**margarine**
¼ tsp. pepper	**milk, to desired**
1 tsp. baking powder	**consistency**

Put meat, salt and onion in large pot. Add enough water to cover 1-2 inches over meat, then bring to a boil. When meat is cooked, take out and set aside to cool. Keep stock in same pot. Separate meat from bone and add back to stock. Bring to a boil. In separate bowl, combine dumpling ingredients. Add dumpling mixture a tablespoon at a time to pot while keeping stock and meat at a boil. When dumplings and soup stock are thickened, serve.

Sherry Elson
Lansford, North Dakota

Miscellaneous

Froggin'

by Paul Moore
(reprinted courtesy of *Outdoor Oklahoma*, official publication of
the Oklahoma Department Of Wildlife Conservation)

Probably everyone remembers their first time; it stands out
as a milestone. I was a teenager growing up near a major
metropolitan area. The setting of my first "experience" is now a
developed suburb, but then it was open fields, drainage canals,
ditches and ponds—a wild area devoid of interfering human
traffic. We had the area to ourselves most of the time.

While driving, my partner talked about the potential
experience, and my excitement grew. Sure enough, we had a
great time. It was an event that changed my life—froggin'.

The plan was simple. My partner and one of his buddies would
walk on either side of one of the canals with archery equipment
in hand. I was the designated flashlight toter. As the sun set, we
began our quest. My flashlight's beam scanned both banks of

the ditch searching for the telltale, green eyes. Whenever a pair of eyes was located, an arrow would quickly be sent on its way. Luckily, for the frogs anyway, my accomplices weren't too skilled with bows then. I don't remember how many frogs we caught, but I do remember the excitement of the evening, in spite of returning home smelly, wet, muddy and lumpy from the mosquito bites.

Today, in much of the South, froggin' is still popular. In Oklahoma (which I call home), we are blessed with thousands of acres of ponds, creeks, rivers and lakes. For the serious frogger, things couldn't be better. In most states where frogs are legal game there are liberal limits and long seasons. In Oklahoma we can take 30 legs per day (15 frogs). There are many ways to hunt bullfrogs and many devotees of each method.

As mentioned earlier, archery was my first exposure to bullfrogging. Generally, it's not a solitary event. One person shoots while the other is the spotter and flashlight holder. It's nearly impossible and quite unsafe to shoot a bow and hold a flashlight at the same time. I have seen guys with lights attached to their bows and others with miner-type lights on their hats. Smart froggers always take at least one buddy along. You never know when you'll need a hand stepping out of the mud. And, besides, you can make him carry all the frogs.

Equipment for bow froggin' is almost the same as equipment for bowfishing. Fiberglass arrows are recommended for several reasons. First, the arrows are durable. (When shooting at frogs, even the best shooters will bury an arrow in the roots and rocks along the banks.) Glass arrows also allow line attachment for easy retrieval. Barbed tips are also recommended. They'll hold a frog and prevent it from slipping off the end of an arrow. If you're an accomplished bowhunter, you may prefer to use regular arrows with field points. An accurate shot will pin a frog to the bank for easy retrieval.

Gigging is another popular method of collecting bullfrogs. Gigs can be purchased at nearly any sporting goods or hardware store. Many of them come without a pole—just a 3- or 4-pronged gighead. Almost any handle will do, but, generally, the longer the better. A broom handle will do the trick but a 6- or 7-foot piece of PVC tubing is even better. Gigging is a basic concept. Giggers can wade, walk the shore or hunt from a boat. If you use a boat, stability is a concern. Again, spotlighting frogs usually takes a partner. The person with the gig should ease up as close as he can. Usually, the middle of the pole or handle is held with the left hand and the upper end held with the right. When the barbed gig is close enough, thrust the pole forward. If you're lucky, you've got a frog on a stick. With a little practice, almost anyone can master gigging.

Noodlin' or grabbing the frog is the most basic method. This is probably the most exciting and challenging way to go after froglegs. It can be done with or without gloves. Again, illuminate the frog with your flashlight, sneak up on it and just grab. When grabbin' for frogs, make sure it's a frog you are sticking your hand on. (There are some cantankerous critters in those wetlands, too.) A long-handled landing net can also be used for bullfrogs.

In Oklahoma, a very popular method of frogging is with a rod and reel. Frogs will try to stuff just about anything into their mouths, which is to an angler's advantage. One popular bait is a piece of red cloth attached to a hook. Plastic worms also work well and are probably the easiest bait to use. Just cast or swing your bait out past a frog and let it sit there for a few seconds. Draw the bait a little closer to the frog and stop again. (Alternate twitching and resting your bait.) As the bait moves close to the frog, the frog will attack it. If you are using a plastic worm, it will take a few seconds for the frog to stuff it all into its mouth. Finally, set the hook and prepare for a challenging fight. A bullfrog can be as belligerent as any fish you'll ever hook. And, its unpredictability is amazing. It might instantly dive to the pond's bottom and wrap around a submerged root or stump, or it may head inland in leaps that would make Carl Lewis envious.

In some states, firearms may also be used for taking bullfrogs; however, extreme care must be taken. Bullets can ricochet. For safety's sake, hunt only along shorelines with high banks to serve as a backstop. When using firearms for frogs, a hunting license is required. For all other methods, a fishing license is needed. Most frogging is done after dark.

A frog's eyes usually appear a distinctive green to yellowish-green color when a flashlight beam is sent in their direction. When hit with a strong light, frogs freeze in a hypnotic trance, as long as the beam isn't broken. This allows a grabber or gigger to get in close.

When you go frogging, you're going to get wet and muddy. Waders are fine. However, because the best frogging situations occur in warm months, waders can be hot and uncomfortable. An old pair of tennis shoes and long pants will do fine. (Don't forget insects are attracted to lights so long sleeves and plenty of insect repellant will make an outing more enjoyable.)

Mankind has probably been hunting frogs for thousands of years. Even today, it's a sport that technology has overlooked because harvesting methods have barely advanced. When a modern day frogger releases an arrow, thrusts a gig, lowers a net, wiggles a baited hook or grabs with his hands, he's gathering food much the same way his predecessors did thousands of years ago. It's another fine outdoors' tradition that continues.

BBQ Beaver

Serves: 8-10
Prep Time: 2 hours, 30 minutes

> **beaver back legs and
> backstraps (remove fat
> and bones)
> your favorite barbecue
> sauce**
> **3 cans tomato paste
> onions, chopped**
> **½ cup brown sugar**
> **¼ cup lemon juice**
> **1 tsp. chili powder
> salt and pepper to taste**

Simmer beaver until very tender. Discard liquid. Finely chop or shred beaver, removing all membranes and gristle. Prepare sauce with remaining ingredients. Add cooked beaver to sauce and bake 2 hours on low heat (approximately 300 degrees). Serve over buns.

Don Latimer
Delta Junction, Alaska

Froglegs Delicacy

Serves: varies
Prep Time: 20 minutes

**froglegs
your favorite batter
cooking oil**

Remove rear froglegs from frog's hips. Skin along edge of cut with pliers and peel back off at joint. Remove white tendon before cooking. Prepare your favorite batter. Dip froglegs in batter and fry in hot cooking oil.

Paul Moore
Oklahoma City, Oklahoma

BBQ Raccoon

Serves: 8
Prep Time: 4-6 hours

1 raccoon, quartered	**1 T. lemon pepper**
1 tsp. salt	**1 16-oz. bottle barbecue**
1 tsp. black pepper	**sauce**
1 tsp. red pepper	**1 large onion, chopped**
1 tsp. oregano	**1 tsp. garlic powder**

In large pot, cover raccoon with water. Add salt and boil until meat is tender. Remove meat; set aside to cool. Remove meat from bones. Transfer meat into baking pan. Mix remaining ingredients with meat; cover with foil. Place meat on rack over hot hickory or oak coals in pit. Smoke for 2 hours.

Neil Means
Spurger, Texas

Honey-Baked Potatoes And Coon

Serves: 4-6
Prep Time: 1-2 hours

1 coon, cut up	**5 potatoes, peeled and**
1/2 cup honey	**chunked**
1 tsp. mustard powder	**6 carrots, chunked**
2 T. garlic salt	**3 celery stalks, chopped**
1 T. salt	

Combine honey, mustard powder, garlic salt and salt. Baste coon in 11 1/2x17-inch pan with honey mixture. Bake at 350 degrees for 45 minutes to 1 hour, basting every 15 minutes. Add potatoes, carrots and celery. Still basting every 15 minutes, bake for another 45 minutes or until meat is tender.

Dwayne Warner Sr.
Yucca Valley, California

Raccoon With Sauerkraut

Serves: 4-6
Prep Time: 2-3 hours

**3-4 lbs. raccoon pieces,
fat and glands
removed**
1 T. flour
**1 can sauerkraut, rinsed
and drained**
**1 large tart apple, cored
and chopped**
1/2 cup chicken broth
**1/4 cup brown sugar,
packed**
1/2 tsp. caraway seed
1 bay leaf
**2 T. Worcestershire
sauce**
1/2 tsp. salt
1/2 tsp. paprika
1/8 tsp. pepper
**6 small baking potatoes,
halved**

Preheat oven to 350 degrees. Add flour to large (14x20-inch)
cooking bag; shake to distribute. Place bag in 2-inch, deep
roasting pan; set aside. In medium mixing bowl, combine
sauerkraut, apple, chicken broth, brown sugar and caraway
seed; mix well. Spoon into cooking bag. Add bay leaf. In small
bowl, combine Worcestershire sauce, salt, paprika, and
pepper. Brush sauce over raccoon pieces. Arrange raccoon
pieces over sauerkraut mixture. Add potato halves. Close
cooking bag with nylon tie. Make six, 1/2-inch slits in top of bag.
Bake until raccoon pieces are tender. Discard bay leaf before
serving.

Robert Shenk
Columbia, Pennsylvania

Cranberry Braised Raccoon

Serves: 3-4
Prep Time: 2-3 hours

2½ lbs. raccoon pieces, fat and glands removed
1 cup cranberries, finely chopped
1 cup apple cider
¼ cup honey
1 tsp. orange peel, grated
¾ tsp. salt
⅛ tsp. ground cloves
⅛ tsp. ground nutmeg

Place raccoon pieces in large saucepan. In small mixing bowl, combine remaining ingredients; mix well. Pour mixture over raccoon pieces. Heat to boiling. Reduce heat; cover. Simmer until raccoon is tender, stirring once or twice.

Robert Shenk
Columbia, Pennsylvania

Raccoon Ala Edible

Serves: 4-6
Prep Time: 1-2 hours

2 raccoons, remove fat and glands
green peppers, chopped
onions, chopped
carrots, chunked
potatoes, chunked
3 cans cream of mushroom soup

Cut raccoon meat into pieces. Put meat into pot and boil until meat comes off bones. Change water in pot once or twice while boiling to remove fat juices. Place meat into pan and add green peppers, onions, carrots and potatoes. Stir in condensed soup. Cover and cook in oven until vegetables are done.

George York
Woodbury, Connecticut

Rattlesnake

Serves: 2-4
Prep Time: 1-2 hours

1 rattlesnake	**3 large eggs**
¼ cup olive oil	**⅛ cup Italian seasoning**
½ cup cooking oil	**salt and pepper to taste**
3-4 cups bread crumbs, crushed	**1 cup marsala cooking wine**

Cut snake into chunks. Put olive oil and cooking oil in large, cast-iron skillet. Set stove for 170-185 degrees. Dip snake into egg, then roll in bread crumbs; place in hot oil. Once snake starts to cook, sprinkle Italian seasoning and salt and pepper on it. Add marsala cooking wine. Cover and simmer.

Bruce Miller
Sumner, Iowa

Texas Rattlesnake Chili

Serves: 6
Prep Time: 2 hours, 30 minutes

1 cup rattlesnake, cubed	**1 tsp. ground cayenne pepper**
1 lb. ground beef, lean	**2 T. chili powder**
2 T. cooking oil	**8 cups tomatoes, undrained**
½ cup onion, chopped	**⅔ cup tomato paste**
½ cup green pepper, chopped	**2 cups water**
2 garlic cloves, minced	**2 cups pasta, uncooked**
2 tsp. salt	

In 5-qt. saucepan, heat oil and cook onion, green pepper and garlic until tender. Add meat and cook until done, about 5 minutes. Stir in seasonings, tomatoes and tomato paste. Heat to boiling, then simmer for 2 hours. Before serving, add water and return chili to boiling. Stir in uncooked pasta and continue boiling (stirring frequently) for 10-15 minutes.

Ken Powell
Kenosha, Wisconsin

Drunken Snapper

Serves: 3-4
Prep Time: 6 hours, 30 minutes

3-4 lbs. snapping turtle
   meat, cut up
   salt and pepper to taste
   garlic powder to taste
2/3 cup shortening
3/4 cup beer

1 medium onion, halved
3 medium potatoes,
   halved

Lightly season meat with salt, pepper and garlic powder. Roll meat in flour. Place meat in greased skillet and brown. Pour beer in Crockpot. Add browned meat. (Crockpot should be set on high.) Boil onion for 15 minutes; then place in Crockpot. Boil potatoes for 10 minutes; then place in Crockpot. Cook for 6 hours. Serve alone or with noodles.

Eric Grove
Nappanee, Indiana

Sweet And Sour Woodchuck

Serves: 4
Prep Time: 8-10 hours

1 medium woodchuck
   salt and pepper to taste
1/4 cup brown sugar
1/4 cup vinegar
1/4 cup soy sauce
1/4 cup chili sauce

Cut woodchuck into serving-size pieces. Season meat with salt and pepper and place in Crockpot. Mix remaining ingredients together and pour over woodchuck. Cover and set on low heat. Let cook for 8-10 hours. Delicious!

John Whitney
New Paltz, New York

Index

SNIPE
Snipe On Toast, 140

SQUIRREL
Baked Gray Squirrel, 194
Bushy Tail Stew, 194
Carl's Squirrels, 198
Fricasseed Squirrel, 195
Fried Squirrel, 197
Russ's Sauteed Squirrel, 197
Squirrel And Dumplings, 96
Squirrel And Gravy, 196
Squirrel And Rabbit
　Dumplings, 198
Squirrel Au Vin, 196
Squirrel Brunswick Stew, 97
Stew With Dumplings, 193
Succulent Squirrel, 195

TURKEY
BBQ Turkey Loaf, 140
Gas-Grilled Wild Turkey, 142
Roasted Wild Turkey & Corn
　Bread Dressing, 100
Smoked Wild Turkey, 99
Turkey Cabbage Rolls, 141

TURTLE
Drunken Snapper, 208

VENISON
4th Of July Special Ribs, 29
Adirondack Meatloaf, 27
Anna's Meatloaf Madness, 25
Apple Venison Balls, 104
Arm's Camp Steaks, 39
Australian Rissoles, 66
Bagged Venison, 34
Bailey Venison Stroganoff, 45
Baked Venison Heart, 106
Barbecued Deer Chops, 18
Barbecued Venison Meatloaf, 26
Batter-Dipped Meatballs, 112
BBQ Deer Jerky, 23
BBQ Venison Ribs, 30
Bennie Bits, 40
Blue Cheese Venison Burgers, 49
Boneless Venison Roast, 31
Brandy Pepper Steak With

Radishes, 40
Breaded Venison Fingersteaks, 57
Brown Venison Stew, 44
Buck Kabobs, 68
Buttermilk-Dipped Venison
　Fingers, 107
Cajun Venison Meatloaf, 24
Cajun Venison Subs, 62
Camper's Venison, 110
Charbroiled Venison Chops, 20
Chicago Chili, 13
Chili, 17
Colorado Ranch Roast, 34
Country-Fried Venison Steaks
　And Gravy, 110
Crockpot Venison Roast, 32
Cross Creek Hollow Jerky, 114
Cross Creek Hollow Tender
　Roast, 111
Cubed Venison Chili, 16
Danner Deer Jerky, 24
Deer Camp Bean Chili, 17
Deer Hearts, 77
Deer Hunter's Roast, 32
Deer In Tears, 64
Deer Jerky, 22
Deer On A Spear, 71
Deer Pot Pie, 82
Deer Steaks, 35
Deer Summer Sausage, 55
Deer Supreme, 38
Dilly Venison Stew, 43
Dried Venison, 71
Easy Deer Chops, 19
Easy Venison Chili, 16
Game Heart, 76
Ground Venison Supreme, 60
Hearty Venison Bake, 52
Hot & Spicy Jerky, 22
Ida's Venison Cacciatore, 50
Italian Venison Meatballs, 28
Jerky, 21
Joe And Joshua's Venison
　Delight, 41
Kevin's Deer Jerky, 23
King's Venison Yaki-Tori, 50
Klinck's Venison Pancakes, 70
Leg Of Venison, 63
Little Meat Sandwiches, 69

Contributing Members

Bacon, Tim
  Fort Dodge, IA, 15, 28
Bailey, Mr. and Mrs. B.R.
  Elizabethtown, PA, 45, 61
Barry, Chuck
  Houston, TX, 180
Behrens, Fritz
  Anderson, IN, 192
Bender, Robert
  Chambersburg, PA, 123, 133
Benson, James
  Haines, AK, 35
Ber, Richard
  Austin, TX, 14, 59
Bisso, Robert
  Memphis, TN, 57, 175
Blanda, Paul
  Charlestown, RI, 28, 148
Boeselager, Mike
  Maribel, WI, 181
Bolick, Jack
  Payson, AZ, 160
Bolton, Russ
  Griffin, GA, 197
Boomgaarden, Irvin
  Trent, SD, 29
Bradybaugh, James
  Ontario, NY, 47
Brennan, Ashley
  Garrison, NY, 64
Brienza, Robert
  Scotia, NY, 33, 77, 78
Brought, Kirby
  Middleburg, PA, 140, 188
Brown, Jerry
  Union Lake, MI, 23
Burke, John
  Philadelphia, PA, 178
Burke, Peter
  Modesto, CA, 175
Campbell, Richard
  Tamaqua, PA, 18
Cooper, Rick
  Vienna, OH, 32, 44
Cover, Frank
  Dunstable, MA, 43
Crowther, Dave
  Bluemont, VA, 62, 65,
  69, 71, 165

Cuipenski, Pete
  New Port Richey, FL, 34
Danner, Lesa
  Woodstock, VA, 24
Davies, John
  Hanover, MD, 64
Davis, Floyd
  Sacramento, CA, 132, 133
Delisle, Daniel
  Haddon Field, NJ, 153
Demilio, Jim
  Spring Lake, MI, 187
Depaolantonio, Joe
  Colorado Springs, CO, 13,
  135, 162
Distel, James
  Philadelphia, PA, 20, 134, 193
Dollinger, DeLane
  Venturia, ND, 131, 156
Elson, Sherry
  Lansford, ND, 82, 198
Evans, R.W.
  Wheaton, IL, 31
Foldenauer, Gerald
  King Cove, AK, 177
Gailey, Robert
  Nezperce, ID, 35, 187
Gay, Charles
  Pierson, FL, 45, 159
Giaccio, Ralph
  Renton, WA, 155
Gobiasky, John
  Lake Huntington, NY, 27, 34
Gonzalez, Deane
  Honolulu, HI, 126, 152
Greeno, Dick
  Lowell, MA, 127, 174
Gregorich, Lewis
  Bessemer, PA, 44
Grove, Eric
  Nappanee, IN, 196, 208
Gutierrez, Dave
  Stratford, VA, 167
Hansen, Philip Dyhre
  Cliffside Park, NJ, 131, 151
Hargett, Edward
  Columbus, GA, 193
Haydysch, Kenneth
  Crystal Lake, IL, 58, 59

SEND US YOUR GAME RECIPE

Title: _____

Serves: _____

Prep Time: _____

Ingredients:

_____
_____
_____
_____
_____
_____
_____
_____
_____

Directions:

_____ fold here
_____
_____
_____
_____
_____
_____
_____
_____
_____
_____
_____
_____
_____
_____
_____
_____
_____

Your NAHC Member # _____
Your Name _____
Address _____
City/State/Zip _____

North American Hunting Club
P.O. Box 3401
Minneapolis, MN 55343

(tape or staple here)

SEND US YOUR GAME RECIPE

Title: _____

Serves: _____

Prep Time: _____

Ingredients:

_____
_____
_____
_____
_____
_____
_____
_____

Directions:

_____ fold here
_____
_____
_____
_____
_____
_____
_____
_____
_____
_____
_____
_____
_____
_____
_____
_____

Your NAHC Member # _____

Your Name _____

Address _____

City/State/Zip _____

North American Hunting Club
P.O. Box 3401
Minneapolis, MN 55343

(tape or staple here)

A Great Gift Idea...
The NAHC Wild Game Cookbook!

Order extra copies of the 1993 Cookbook for
your friends and family. They make great gifts
—fun to read and practical as well!

You'll also like to have a second copy to keep
at the cabin or in with your camping gear.

Send your order in now and get yours at the
special Member's price of only $9.95 each.
(Non-members pay $14.95)

Send me _____ copies of the 1993 Wild Game Cookbook.
I'm enclosing $9.95 each (non-members pay $14.95).
Include $1.50 per order for Postage and Handling.

If paying by Check or Money Order, send this form in
an envelope with your payment to: NAHC Cookbook,
P.O. Box 3402, Minneapolis, MN 55343.
Charge customers may cut out this page, fold and mail.
(Don't forget to put on a stamp)

☐ Check here if you'd like to receive information about
ordering NAHC Wild Game Cookbooks from past years.

| Payment Method:
___Check or M.O.
___MasterCard
___Visa | Card # _____
Exp. Date_____
Signature_____ |

Name_____Member # _____
Address_____
City/State/Zip_____

CB93

North American Hunting Club
P.O. Box 3401
Minneapolis, MN 55343

(tape or staple here)

Hunters belong in the NAHC ...
and it's so *simple* to join!
Cut out, fold and mail the card below.

- *North American Hunter* magazine
- *Keeping Track* member news
- Swap Hunts with fellow members
- Hunting Reports on guides/outfitters
- *Approved Outfitters & Guides* booklet
- Free Hunts Contest
- New Product & Field Test Reports
- Products & Service Discounts
- Access to Club land
- Your photo in "Member Shots"
- Big Game Awards, and much, much more!

fold here

ENROLLMENT FORM

Count me in . . .

I want to increase my hunting skills and pleasure.

Here are my $18 annual dues for membership in the North American Hunting Club. I understand my membership will start immediately upon receipt of this application and continue for 12 months.

Name _____
PLEASE PRINT

Address _____

City _____ State _____ Zip _____

Check One:

☐ Check for $18 enclosed

☐ Bill my Master Card/VISA

Credit Card No._____ Exp. Date_____

Signature_____

93 WGCB

If recommended by current member:

Name _____ NAHC No._____

BUSINESS REPLY CARD
FIRST CLASS   PERMIT NO. 17619   MPLS., MN

POSTAGE WILL BE PAID BY ADDRESSEE

North American Hunting Club
P.O. Box 3402
Minneapolis, MN 55343

(tape or staple here)